CW00970460

Palgrave Studies in Global Citizenship Education and Democracy

Series Editor
Jason Laker
San Jose State University
San Jose, CA, USA

This series will engage with the theoretical and practical debates regarding citizenship, human rights education, social inclusion, and individual and group identities as they relate to the role of higher and adult education on an international scale. Books in the series will consider hopeful possibilities for the capacity of higher and adult education to enable citizenship, human rights, democracy and the common good, including emerging research and interesting and effective practices. It will also participate in and stimulate deliberation and debate about the constraints, barriers and sources and forms of resistance to realizing the promise of egalitarian Civil Societies. The series will facilitate continued conversation on policy and politics, curriculum and pedagogy, review and reform, and provide a comparative overview of the different conceptions and approaches to citizenship education and democracy around the world.

More information about this series at
http://www.palgrave.com/gp/series/14625

Namrata Sharma

Value-Creating Global Citizenship Education

Engaging Gandhi, Makiguchi, and Ikeda as Examples

Namrata Sharma
Ann Arbor, MI, USA

Palgrave Studies in Global Citizenship Education and Democracy
ISBN 978-3-319-78243-0 ISBN 978-3-319-78244-7 (eBook)
https://doi.org/10.1007/978-3-319-78244-7

Library of Congress Control Number: 2018936584

Printed on acid-free paper

This Palgrave Pivot imprint is published by the registered company Springer International Publishing AG part of Springer Nature
The registered company address is: Gewerbestrasse 11, 6330 Cham, Switzerland

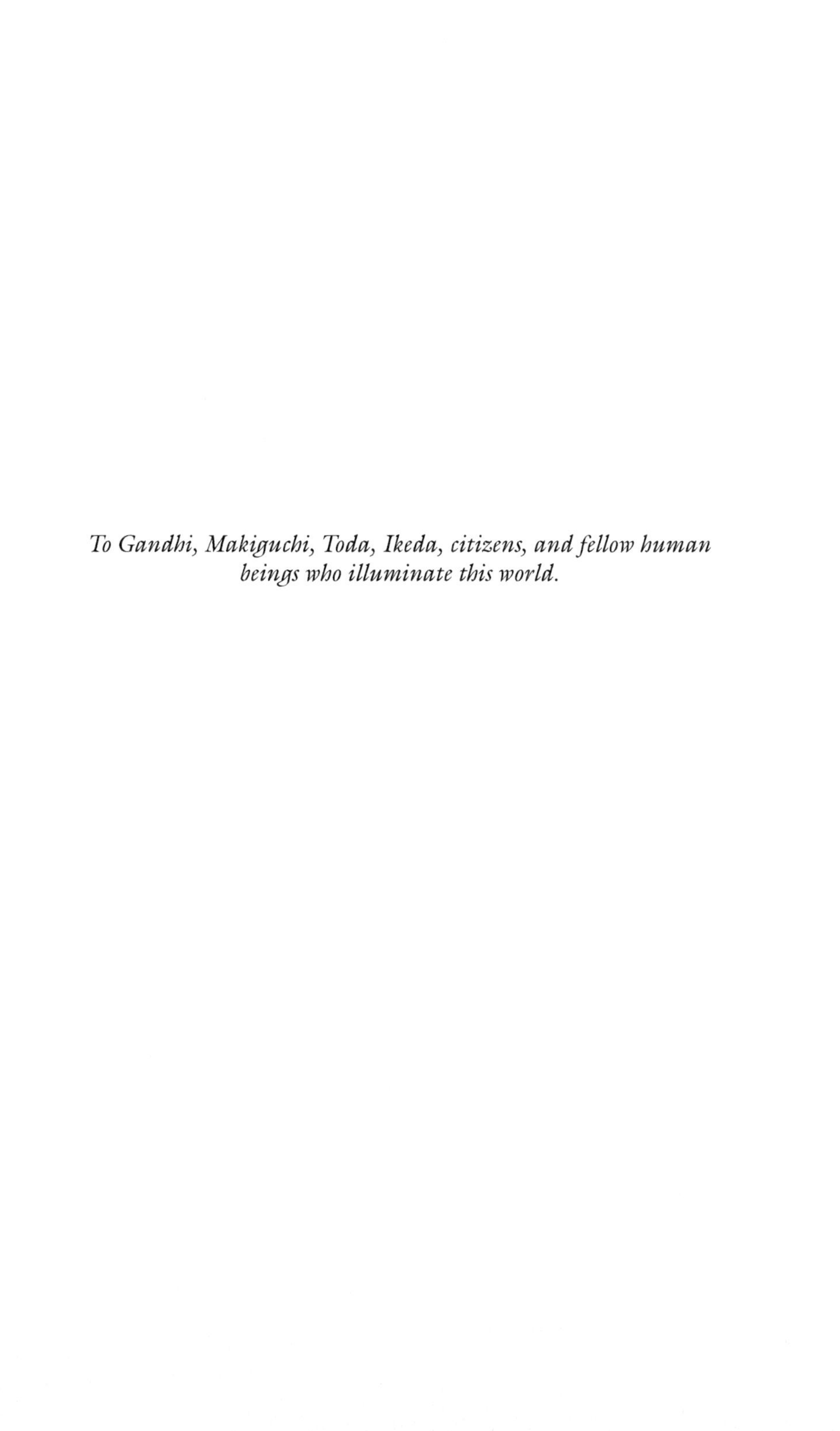

To Gandhi, Makiguchi, Toda, Ikeda, citizens, and fellow human beings who illuminate this world.

Preface

In the past two decades, my work has largely concentrated on education for citizenship through a study of Asian dissidents and leaders of the largest mass movements of their respective countries in recent history. These include the Japanese thinkers Tsunesaburo Makiguchi (1871–1944) and Daisaku Ikeda (b. 1928), and the Indian political leader Mahatma Gandhi (1869–1948). In the more recent past, there has been a surge of studies in the English speaking world that examine the relevance of Ikeda's *soka* or value-creating education to contemporary education, human rights, and a sustainable future. Ikeda, who is the leader of the lay Buddhist organization, the Soka Gakkai, is also a prolific writer, poet, and founder of several institutions promoting peace, culture, and education across 192 countries and territories.

Parallel to the development of *soka*/Ikeda studies is the emerging field of global citizenship education. Some scholars have been interested to examine the relevance of Ikeda's work to the discourse on global citizenship education. Such as, analyze Ikeda's support (as a citizen) to the United Nations and his aim to foster global citizens as the founder of Soka education institutions.

Interestingly, both fields have similar challenges along with their desired contributions. Existing and emerging scholars, practitioners are struggling to bring some order to the disarray in understanding key concepts, thoughts, themes, and perspectives. Further, the discourse in both fields is largely dominated by those situated in North America, Western Europe, and Australia. Although significant work has been done within

Makiguchi studies in Japan, and more recently in China and Taiwan, much of the primary literature on the thinker's educational pedagogy, *Soka kyoikugaku taikei* or The System of Value-Creating Pedagogy, written in Japanese, and secondary source writings in Japanese and Chinese are largely inaccessible due to the language barrier and thereby does not directly inform much of the work being done within Anglophone theoretical and empirical literature, except through the existing and where possible within ongoing translation studies.

In addition, within both global citizenship education and *soka* studies, attempts are being made to bridge the gap between research and praxis (largely through research studies mapping out practice within schools). The shared noble intent for those engaged in both fields is to nurture human beings who, while being rooted in their local communities are concerned with global issues that confront humanity. There is also the common ambition to develop capacity within students who can contribute to the global economy. The overarching attempt within global citizenship education and *soka*/Ikeda studies is largely to promote global consciousness through an education that also meets national standards of competencies.

While this book speaks to those who might be interested in both *soka*/Ikeda studies and global citizenship education, the discussions are primarily aimed to contribute to the emerging discourse within global citizenship education through the non-Western examples of Makiguchi, Gandhi, and Ikeda. It challenges the reader to re-examine research and praxis in global citizenship education (entrenched in a Western paradigm) through the lenses of these selected Asian thinkers. The various questions posited in this book are also aimed at accomplishing this task. It is with the hope to draw the reader to engage in the two contributions that this book attempts to make through a study of these thinkers. Bringing Gandhi into our conversations is particularly relevant to both these aspects. First, their perspectives although situated in non-Western historical contexts are also rooted in an existential dialogue with the West. A historical comparative study of their ideas can make important contributions to the existing discourse in global citizenship education. The second is that the examples of movements that motivate people to take positive action within their respective societies are embedded with learning that can inform classroom practice in global citizenship education. In addressing these issues this book is aimed at research scholars and practitioners; initial and in-service teachers and teacher educators;

academics and universities that are interested in the debates around the internationalization of higher education, the development of programs and curricula within international and comparative education, development education and global learning, future programs on value-creating education for global citizenship, and across disciplines in higher education including within programs that integrate sustainability issues and social responsibility; as well as civil society organizations promoting global citizenship education.

Ann Arbor, USA Namrata Sharma

Acknowledgements

In remembering those who have passed away, Mr. Toshiaki Mizuhata of Soka School, Tokyo, from whom I learned the art of education, and Prof. Jagdish Gundara of University College London—Institute of Education, who helped me develop the scholarship to take this learning into the world.

This work would not have been possible without the generous time and advice of Prof. Douglas Bourn at University College London—Institute of Education, and Prof. Paul Thompson at the University of Nottingham. Many thanks to my students and colleagues at the State University of New York and Soka University Japan. Also thanks goes to Alpha*Plus* consultancy in UK, to Prof. Jason Goulah and friends at DePaul University, Chicago, and for the great support received from the team at Palgrave Macmillan.

My deepest thanks to my loving parents, my wonderful husband Nandit, friends, and family—Richa, you enthuse me as the embodiment of the Soka spirit and Nividi, you inspired this project and many good things in my life.

Chapter 4 was first published in the *International Journal of Development Education and Global Learning*, volume 3, number 2 (2011), pp. 5–19, Trentham Books Limited, reproduction with permission. Also, Chapter 5 was first published in *Policy Futures in Education* (Sage Journals), volume 13, number 3 (2015), pp. 328–341, DOI: 10.1177/1478210315571215, reproduction with permission. Some modifications have been made to both articles to keep consistency with the arguments, language, and format of this book.

Contents

Abbreviations, Acronyms, Chronology

DFID	Department for International Development
EFA	Education for All
ESD	Education for Sustainable Development
GCE or GCED	Global Citizenship Education
GEFI	Global Education First Initiative
LDP	Liberal Democratic Party
MGIEP	Mahatma Gandhi Institute of Education for Peace and Sustainable Development
PISA	Programme for International Student Assessment
SDF	Self-Defense Forces
SGI	Soka Gakkai International
SDGs	Sustainable Development Goals
OECD	The Organization for Economic Co-operation and Development
UN	United Nations
UNICEF	United Nations Children's Fund
UNESCO	United Nations Educational, Scientific and Cultural Organization
WSSD	World Summit on Sustainable Development

List of Figures

CHAPTER 1

Introduction

Abstract In this book, Sharma develops an educational framework based on Asian perspectives for global citizenship education. *Soka* or value-creating education developed by the Japanese educators, Makiguchi and Ikeda is compared to the ideas of Gandhi, the Indian political leader. This chapter explains the important contributions of this work and describes how these can enhance both the discourse and practice within United Nations Educational, Scientific and Cultural Organization (UNESCO's) guidelines for global citizenship education. For example, there are alternative ways of thinking about ourselves, society, nature, and the universe that can add to the intercultural dimension of global citizenship education. Also, there are valuable lessons to be learned from studies on these thinkers and their respective movements who have been embroiled in the socio-political and educational changes within their own countries.

Keywords Global citizenship education · Asian perspectives
Soka education · Makiguchi · Gandhi · Ikeda

This chapter is an autobiographical journey that maps the developments in fields that are related to the dual aspirations of this book reflected in its title. The first aim is to contribute to the discourse on education for global citizenship, more specifically, the United Nations Educational,

N. Sharma, *Value-Creating Global Citizenship Education*,
Palgrave Studies in Global Citizenship Education and Democracy,
https://doi.org/10.1007/978-3-319-78244-7_1

Scientific and Cultural Organization (UNESCO) led Global Citizenship Education agenda and the Western-dominated paradigm within the field of global citizenship education. For example, scholars, such as Dill (2013: 136) has challenged the "dominant mode of Enlightenment liberalism" and questions whether "the advocates of global citizenship education could do more critical and constructive thinking about the particularities of their universal ambitions."

Further discussions, it must be argued, also need to be centered on how and what must be particularized in schooling for global citizenship within multicultural societies. In addition, the engagement with particularities must be attempted not from the sidelines but through reimagining alternative paradigms, perspectives, and possibilities within global citizenship education.[1] As an illustration, in this book *soka* or value creation is studied with the intent to develop global citizenship education *as* value-creating education. The second aim of this book is to contribute to the study of *soka* education.

Literally "value-creating," *soka* is a Japanese approach to curriculum that emerged in 1930s Japan in response to an increasingly militaristic educational system focused on creating subjects of the state rather than contributive citizens of local and global communities. Stressing academic achievement, character development, interdependence, global citizenship, dialogue, and profound student–teacher relationships for social-self actualization and a meaningful life through the taught and untaught curriculum, *soka* approaches undergird 15 Soka kindergartens, primary and secondary schools, women's college, and universities in seven countries across Asia and the Americas. They inform public and private schools and universities in various countries and are practiced by thousands of educators and school leaders in diverse multicultural and multilingual contexts.[2]

The progenitors of *soka* are the Japanese educators, Tsunesaburo Makiguchi (1871–1944), Josei Toda (1900–1958), and Daisaku Ikeda (b. 1928). Makiguchi and his Indian contemporary, Mohandas Karamchand Gandhi *alias* Mahatma Gandhi (1869–1948) shared similar notions of truth and value. Although Makiguchi, Ikeda, and Gandhi had never met, Ikeda has extensively spoken and written about Makiguchi and Gandhi (examples include, Ikeda 1996, 2008a, b, 2010: 123–133).

In the 1990s, when I first became interested in these thinkers and started research into their broader educational relevance, there was scarcely any academic work available in the Anglophone literature.

Within *soka*/Makiguchi studies Alfred Birnbaum's translated and Bethel's (1989) edited excerpts from Makiguchi's pedagogical work *Soka kyoikugaku taikei* (The System of Value-Creating Pedagogy; 1930–1934) continues to largely be the prevailing text within the Anglophone literature with translations in several other languages. More recently and arguably more substantive translation studies have started to emerge with particular relevance to language and literacy education, international perspectives in education, and curriculum theorizing (see Goulah and Gebert 2009; Goulah 2017). Here it is relevant to reference recent studies on terms such as *soka* and Soka (Goulah and Gebert 2009; Goulah and Ito 2012), and the alternative translations for the Japanese term *ningen kyoiku* that is frequently rendered as "humanistic education" in *soka*/Ikeda studies (Goulah 2010; Goulah and Gebert 2009). These are important contributions in terms of standardizing the use of key terms developed through research studies within the emerging discourse in this field, for example, as described in the following two excerpts.

> The word '*soka*' is a neologism Makiguchi coined, based on Toda's suggestion, for the creation (*sozo*) of value (*kachi*). 'Soka' constitutes the name of the schools Ikeda founded based on his application of Makiguchi's value-creating pedagogy. While the former can point to practices both in and outside the Soka schools, 'Soka education' (sometimes also written as 'Soka Education') is often the English translation of the term (*soka kyoiku*, literally 'value creating education') that Ikeda uses to characterize the educational approach passed down from Makiguchi and Toda and practiced in the Soka schools he founded (e.g., Ikeda 2010). Thus, for distinction's sake, we use Soka education to refer specifically to Ikeda's developed philosophy, practice, and curriculum of value-creating education.
>
> (Goulah and Ito 2012: 60–61)

> Ikeda has used the formula *ningen kyoiku* to describe the educational philosophy and practice that has developed on the basis of Makiguchi's pedagogy (Ikeda 1968, 2006). Literally 'human education,' this phrase could be translated as humanistic, humane, or human/people-centered education; it probably indicates all these aspects.
>
> (Goulah and Gebert 2009: 126)

My academic inquiry into Makiguchi's educational work started during my master's studies at Soka University, Japan (1995–1998) supervised by two leading scholars in this field, Professors Kazunori Kumagai and Shoji Saito. Both scholars are among others in the twentieth century who have written extensively on Makiguchi and his educational ideas in Japanese with some articles in English (examples include, Kumagai 2000; Saito 2010). Further, my experience of and work on the ethos of *soka* has extended from being a student at Soka University; in the interactions with the founder, Ikeda; and through the several visits and observational studies conducted over the years in the Soka Schools in Japan (1995–2005). This time period also overlapped with parallel research studies on Gandhi and his educational ideas that were often guided through discussions with Dr. Radhakrishnan, the former head of Gandhi Smriti and Darshan Samiti in New Delhi, India. My ensuing work with Dr. Dayle Bethel in Kyoto and Hawaii, and my doctoral studies in London initiated the inquiry on the relevance of all three thinkers, Gandhi, Makiguchi, and Ikeda from an intercultural perspective under the guidance of (late) Professor Jagdish Gundạra, UNESCO chair for intercultural education, and Mr. Robert Ferguson, faculty and course leader on the Master's in Media Culture and Communication at the Institute of Education, University of London. Further, my work as a research assistant at the Development Education Research Center (DERC), University College London-Institute of Education (2006–2008) provided the opportunity to work with Professor Douglas Bourn on global education projects and issues concerning youth across the higher education sector. Overall these interactions contributed to developing my work on *soka* and Gandhi studies as contributions to the discourse on global citizenship education.

Reflecting back, I realize that it was unusual for a young woman from India to study Japanese and do a master's degree in education in Japan in the 1990s. Also, it has been less common for Ph.D. candidates to research the educational ideas and relevance of Asian thinkers in academic institutions such as the University of London. However, these decisions were guided by the intent to bring such less widely known thinkers and perspectives that have shown to significantly influence the lives of people and communities into the debates and practice of mainstream education.

More recently, during my time as visiting lecturer at Soka University Japan (2014–2015) and through continued engagement with colleagues in North America, Europe, and India, I find there to be an increase in doctoral studies that are interested to examine the relevance of *soka* studies to debates related to global citizenship education. Some that might be of interest to the readers of this book are *Cosmopolitan Education and the Creation of Value* (Obelleiro 2014), and *Exploration of Soka Education Principles on Global Citizenship: A Qualitative Study of US K-3 Soka Educators* (Takazawa 2016).

To summarize some of the myriad conversations and academic work taking place in this field, in North America there is a growing momentum through the newly established Institute for Daisaku Ikeda Studies in Education at DePaul University, Chicago by Professor Jason Goulah; annual conferences organized by the students at Soka University of America; and existing and ongoing doctoral studies in this field across the US. Some doctoral work is also supported by the Ikeda Center for Peace, Learning and Dialogue, Boston through the Education Fellows Program in which candidates can engage with advisors, who are well-established scholars from across a variety of different fields. Also, over the years there has been a wider presence of *soka* scholars at international conferences in this region, such as at annual meetings of the American Educational Research Association (AERA).

This surge in activities calls for an urgent need to bring together the discourse and practice that has been taking place across countries on Makiguchi, Toda, Ikeda, and *soka* as a pedagogical, philosophical, and curricular approach. There is also the opportunity to address the paucity of research and discourse on the sociological impact of Soka, for instance, as a socio-political construct. For example, Dobblelaere and Wilson's study (1994) suggests that the members of the Soka Gakkai International in the UK show a greater degree of involvement in socio-political affairs than the sample taken from the general UK population, which requires a more detailed analysis through further research. Also, Fisker-Nielsen's (2012) sustained research conducted in Japan and UK, on the engagement of Soka within Japanese politics and its relation to youth and education is particularly noteworthy.

Broadening the discussion, with relevance to the field of global citizenship education, requires an examination of the educational impact of Soka as a movement. It is comparable to Gandhi's *satyagraha*[3] as an attempt to create social change at a grassroots level through uniting a disparate body politic. There are several reasons as to why historically ordinary citizens become embroiled within the affairs of their local communities, including through an appeal to the individual's interests, values, and concerns. Further, since the turn of this century and particularly with recent events, such as in the Middle East that are inspired by "wired citizenship" there is an urgent need, as Torres (2017) suggests, to build global citizenship education as a global social movement. Within this proposed new discourse the lessons from the progenitors of *soka* and *satyagraha* are particularly significant to make creative contributions.

This work borrows from my earlier studies in this field that began with a comparative analysis of the educational ideas of Makiguchi and Gandhi as *Value Creators in Education* (Sharma 1999). Moving ahead, I became interested in their dissimilar fates. To explain, Gandhi who was revered as the *Mahatma* or "great soul" during his own life had no noticeable influence in India shortly after his death. There are several reasons as to why Gandhi's ideas were largely disregarded after his death, including the differences in political judgments between him and his successor, the first Prime Minister of independent India, Jawaharlal Nehru (1889–1964). As a youth growing up in India I had scarcely any knowledge of Gandhi. This was very different from my experience whilst studying at Soka University, of the growing influence of Makiguchi and Ikeda in Japan (see Sharma 2008: vii–x for details). Consequently, in a subsequent work, I examined the use and influence of *Makiguchi and Gandhi–Their Educational Relevance for the 21st Century* (Sharma 2008).

In the twentieth and twenty-first centuries, while scholarly work on Makiguchi has continued to expand in Japan and abroad, not much work has been done in English on Toda during this period. Although, some significant work has started within the new Master's program on Value-Creating Education for Global Citizenship at DePaul University. Substantial work however, is underway on the relevance of Ikeda's views for contemporary education, which arguably in effect also sheds light on the creativity of Toda. In numerous writings, Ikeda attributes much of his learning to Toda who rigorously mentored him through "a curriculum of history, literature, philosophy, economics, science and organization theory" (Ikeda 2008a: 448–449).

As a mentor himself, Ikeda in many ways compares well with Gandhi. Although separated by time, both thinkers have displayed ingenuity, creativity, and boldness in enthusing people within and across diverse societies to participate in their respective politics, education, and society. A study of these leaders and their movements is especially relevant to the debates on education for citizenship in modern nation states experiencing the effects of migration, displacement, and transition.

The main question that guides this work is, "what contributions can be identified through a contextual and historical analysis of Makiguchi, Gandhi, and Ikeda for global citizenship education?" In responding to the call for supplementary perspectives that have been made within recent studies that are a critique of the dominant Western-neoliberal paradigm (Andreotti n.d., 2006; Dill 2013; Merryfield 2009; Tarozzi and Torres 2016), this book develops an educational framework based on the selected Asian perspectives that aims to expand the current focus within global citizenship education from individual empowerment to a collective effort to tackle global issues. This is whilst being aware that all too often simplistic contrasts are made between notions of individualistic versus collectivist, Western versus Eastern perspectives. For example, a study of these thinkers shows a broad range of influences that have impacted their lives and work.

A shift in paradigm and perspectives it is argued here, will have a significant bearing on the praxis and the three domains of learning within the global citizenship education conceptual dimensions of UNESCO—the cognitive, socio-emotional, and behavioral (UNESCO 2015: 14–15). These correspond to the four pillars of learning described in the Delors Report (1996, see also UNESCO 2001) *Learning: The treasure within*, that are, learning to know, to do, to be and to live together. This book develops a framework for practice based on these UNESCO guidelines and through a study of the Asian thinkers that can be used as a resource for global citizenship education among others recommended by UNESCO (2015). The two contributions it makes are, first, there are alternative ways of thinking about ourselves, society, nature, and the universe that can add to the intercultural dimension of global citizenship education. Second, these selected thinkers were embroiled in the socio-political and educational changes within their respective countries. There are several lessons that can be learned from their examples, such as the political implications of taking action based on one's values and beliefs.

This book wrestles with the above issues to situate their relevance and offers practical suggestions for teachers and curriculum developers, as well as policy makers. The attempt is to contribute to theory and praxis in global citizenship education through non-Western perspectives. As a result, there are two parts to this book that engage respectively with the theoretical foundations (in Part 1), and the practical application of this study to teaching global citizenship education (in Part 2).

The first part builds on previous theoretical and comparative research work on the selected thinkers. Chapter 2 explains why a comparison is made between these chosen thinkers and its relevance to the aims of this book. It engages with the Asian thinkers' core ideas, modes of thinking, strategies, behaviors, and beliefs as active protagonists in their respective countries. Chapter 3 contributes to the aim of *learning to know*. It engages in a discussion on what should be part of the learning experience. For example, it is argued that the curriculum ought to be non-centric, that is, represent intercultural perspectives that include different ways of thinking about ourselves, society, nature, and the universe. It could select from the knowledge and wisdom of diverse peoples and communities, and expand the focus within global citizenship education from individual empowerment to an emphasis on a collective effort to create value for self and others. Chapter 4 discusses issues related to the goal of *learning to be* from a study of selected Asian perspectives that develop a sense of interdependence and common humanity, and enhance dialogic, reflective, and transformative learning experiences. In relation to this, it examines the contributions that Ikeda's ideas can make to revisit the notion of dialogue in global citizenship education. Chapter 5 explores the aspect of *learning to do* and involves a critical analysis of what it means to be an active citizen. For instance, a study of these thinkers shows that while it is important to enable students to behave effectively and responsibly, it is also relevant that they consider the political implications of taking action based on values, such as peace and non-violence. As discussed in this chapter, paradoxes and contradictions often emerge when one takes action in real-world politics, and there are merits in studying about these and other controversial issues within the classroom. This chapter develops questions for classroom teaching from the study of these three thinkers and provides segue into the next part of this book.

The second part of this book engages with the praxis. Chapters 6 and 7 are practice chapters which discuss the implications for *learning to live together* and emphasize the need to build relationships through the practice of value-creating global citizenship education–between the student and the learning material, student and teacher, other students, the community, and the wider world. Chapter 6 brings together the various themes that were developed in the previous chapters for a practice of global citizenship education with the addition of climate change. The proposed six themes are, (i) a sense of interdependence, common humanity, and a global outlook; (ii) an awareness of climate change as planetary citizens; (iii) a commitment to reflective, dialogic, and transformative learning; (iv) a commitment to sustainable development through intercultural perspectives; (v) a belief in the value-creating capacity for social-self actualization; and (vi) an understanding of peace and non-violence as being central to the human rights agenda. These are relevant to K-12 teaching, and across various subject areas in higher education, as well as within informal and non-formal education. Chapter 7 continues to offer teaching strategies through suggestions made for lessons that engage with Gandhi, Makiguchi, and Ikeda's beliefs, modes of thinking, behaviors, and strategies for action. These are not typical formal lesson plans but include teaching suggestions and guidelines for teacher educators, academics, and practitioners. The concluding Chapter 8 makes suggestions for policy and praxis on *learning the treasure within* based on the various strands and elements discussed in this work.

Notes

1. As suggested for the field of curriculum studies (Schubert 1986).
2. This paragraph was drafted by Prof. Jason Goulah at DePaul University for our jointly facilitated pre-conference session at the American Educational Research Association, 2017.
3. The word *satyagraha* comprises of the two words, *satya* (truth) and *agraha* (insistence or holding firmly to), which put together can be translated as non-violent resistance; a relentless search for truth; truth-force; holding on to truth. It is the term Gandhi used to describe the political movement led by him for India's independence from the British Raj (or rule).

References

Andreotti, V. (2006). Soft versus critical global citizenship education. *Policy & Practice: A Development Education Review, 3*, 40–51.

Andreotti, V. (n.d.). *Engaging the (geo)political economy of knowledge construction: Towards decoloniality and diversality in global citizenship education.* Retrieved from https://www.ucalgary.ca/peacestudies/files/peacestudies/Engaging%20the%20(geo)political%20economy%20of%20knowledge%20construction.pdf.

Bethel, D. M. (Ed.). (1989). *Education for creative living: Ideas and proposals of Tsunesaburo Makiguchi.* Ames: Iowa State University Press.

Delors, J., et al. (1996). *Learning: The treasure within.* Paris: UNESCO.

Dill, J. S. (2013). *The longings and limits of global citizenship education: The modern pedagogy of schooling in a cosmopolitan age.* New York: Routledge.

Dobbelaere, K., & Wilson, B. (1994). *A time to chant: The Soka Gakkai Buddhists in Britain.* Oxford: Clarendon Press.

Fisker-Nielsen, A. M. (2012). *Religion and politics in contemporary Japan: Soka Gakkai youth and Komeito*. Japan Anthropology Workshop Series. London: Routledge.

Goulah, J. (2010). From (harmonious) community life to (creative) coexistence. Considering Daisaku Ikeda's educational philosophy in the Parker, Dewey, Makiguchi and Ikeda "reunion". *Schools: Studies Education, 7*(2), 253–275.

Goulah, J., & Gebert, A. (2009). Tsunesaburo Makiguchi: Introduction to the man, his ideas, and the special issue. *Educational Studies, 45*, 115–132.

Goulah, J., & Ito, T. (2012). Daisaku Ikeda's curriculum of Soka education: Creating value through dialogue, global citizenship, and "human education" in the mentor-disciple relationship. *Curriculum Inquiry, 42*(1), 56–79.

Goulah, J. (Ed.). (2017). *Makiguchi Tsunesaburo in the context of language, identity, and education*. New York: Routledge.

Ikeda, D. (1968). *The human revolution* (Vol. 1). Tokyo: Seikyo Press.

Ikeda, D. (1996). Gandhism and the modern world. In *A new humanism: The university addresses of Daisaku Ikeda* (pp. 128–139). New York: Weatherhill.

Ikeda, D. (2006). *To the youthful pioneers of soka: Lectures, essays and poems on value-creating education*. Tokyo: Soka University Student Union.

Ikeda, D. (2008a). Thoughts on education for global citizenship. In *My dear friends in America: Collected U.S. addresses 1990–1996* (2nd ed.) (pp. 441–451). Santa Monica, CA: World Tribune Press.

Ikeda, D. (2008b). Tsunesaburo Makiguchi's lifelong pursuit of justice and humane values. In *My dear friends in America: Collected U.S. addresses 1990–1996* (pp. 406–419). Santa Monica, CA: World Tribune Press.

Ikeda, D. (2010). *Soka education: For the happiness of the individual* (Rev. ed.). Santa Monica, CA: Middleway Press.

Kumagai, K. (2000). *Tsunesaburo Makiguchi*. Tokyo: Daisanbunmeisha.

Makiguchi, T. ([1930–1934] 1981–1988). *Makiguchi Tsunesaburo zenshu* [The complete works of Makiguchi Tsunesaburo] (Vols. 1–10). Tokyo: Daisan Bunmeisha.

Merryfield, M. (2009). Moving the center of global education: From imperial worldviews that divide the world to double consciousness, contrapuntal pedagogy, hybridity, and cross-cultural competence. In T. F. Kirkwood-Tucker (Ed.), *Visions in global education* (pp. 215–239). New York: Peter Lang.

Obelleiro, G. A. (2014). *Cosmopolitan education and the creation of value*. Unpublished doctoral dissertation, Columbia University, New York.

Saito, S. (2010). *Makiguchi Tsunesaburo no shiso* [The philosophy of Makiguchi Tsunesaburo]. Tokyo: Daisan Bunmeisha.

Schubert, W. H. (1986). *Curriculum: Perspective, paradigm, and possibility*. New York: Macmillan.

Sharma, N. (1999). *Value creators in education: Japanese educator Makiguchi & Mahatma Gandhi and their relevance for the Indian education* (2nd ed.). New Delhi: Regency Publications.

Sharma, N. (2008). *Makiguchi and Gandhi: Their educational relevance for the 21st century*. Lanham, MD: University Press of America and Rowman & Littlefield.

Takazawa, M. (2016). *Exploration of soka education principles on global citizenship: A qualitative study of U.S. K-3 soka educators*. Unpublished doctoral dissertation, University of San Francisco, San Francisco. Retrieved from http://repository.usfca.edu/diss/324.

Tarozzi, M., & Torres, C. A. (2016). *Global citizenship education and the crises of multiculturalism: Comparative perspectives*. London: Bloomsbury Academic.

Torres, C. A. (2017). *Theoretical and empirical foundations of critical global citizenship education*. New York: Routledge.

UNESCO, United Nations Educational Scientific and Cultural Organization International Bureau of Education. (2001). Learning to live together: Have we failed? A seminar of the ideas and contributions arising from the forty-sixth session of UNESCO'S international conference on education. In *Forty-sixth session of UNESCO'S international conference on education*, 5–8 September 2001. Geneva: UNESCO, International Bureau of Education.

UNESCO, United Nations Educational Scientific and Cultural Organization. (2015). *Global citizenship education: Topics and learning objectives*. Paris: UNESCO.

PART I

Theory and Research

CHAPTER 2

Makiguchi, Ikeda, and Gandhi: A Brief Comparative Study

Abstract The focus of this chapter is educational, political, and comparative. This study engages with the Asian thinkers Tsunesaburo Makiguchi, Daisaku Ikeda, and Mahatma Gandhi's core ideas, creative strategies, behaviors, modes of thinking, and beliefs as active protagonists in their respective countries. It reflects on how these thinkers were all motivated to take positive action based on their ideas and values. However, their fates have been dissimilar. One of the reasons for this is whether or not their ideas have been used creatively and directly confront educational challenges and political processes. Enhancing criticality, creativity that can contribute to social-self actualization and bold collective efforts are lessons from this study for the discourse and United Nations Educational, Scientific and Cultural Organization (UNESCO) led practice of *learning to live together* within global citizenship education.

Keywords Learning to live together · Asian perspectives
Soka education · Makiguchi · Gandhi · Ikeda

Introduction

The focus of this chapter is educational, political, and comparative and it begins with the argument that while extensive comparative research has been undertaken in the East and West, there is still a dearth of research

N. Sharma, *Value-Creating Global Citizenship Education*,
Palgrave Studies in Global Citizenship Education and Democracy,
https://doi.org/10.1007/978-3-319-78244-7_2

and literature which develops a broader understanding and compares East with East. This is especially the case within debates on citizenship and intercultural education where the educational policies in the West have not engaged with the practices in the East.[1] However, in many Asian countries, including India, for more than a century there has been a heavy influence of Western authors on citizenship issues (Alston 1910; Gupta et al. 1990).

This chapter casts some light on selected Asian thinkers who have contributed to peace and education: Tsunesaburo Makiguchi (1871–1944) who was an educator in Japan, his successor, Daisaku Ikeda (b. 1928), and the Indian political leader Mahatma Gandhi (1869–1948). It highlights their political and educational creativity by focusing on their contributions at national and international levels and the longer term significance of their respective educational and political ideas.[2] These include Gandhi's influence on the civil rights movement in South Africa and the *chipko* movement in India; and Makiguchi and Ikeda's educational and political impact in Japan and their growing influence worldwide.

This chapter is based on previous comparative studies of the lives and fates of these thinkers (Gundara and Sharma 2008; Sharma 1999, 2008). In one study (Sharma 2008) an interdisciplinary methodology was developed to locate the ideas of such indigenous thinkers, their effectiveness as citizens within their own historical context, and their impact on civic movements both within their own time as well as afterward. In that comparative study on Makiguchi and Gandhi conducted through nearly a decade of research, three historical readings were used to interpret their relevance. First, a history of the era and time in which they lived to provide a contextual setting; second, the specific events and influences that shaped their personal histories and led to the formation of their respective value systems; and the third was concerned with the re-reading of the use of their values within the twenty-first-century context. One of the outcomes of the study was the first comprehensive analysis of the conceptual foundations of Gandhi's values with comparison to Makiguchi's ideas. A similar exhaustive study needs to be undertaken on the significance of Ikeda's life and work.

My prior comparative work (Sharma 1999, 2008) provided detailed examination of the historical actors as well as their influence within their respective countries and selected schools. Some outcomes from these studies are used as relevant in this book.

This historical-comparative study of Makiguchi, Ikeda, and Gandhi is concerned to address sociological, pedagogical, and political issues. The following sections adopt a comparative approach to their ideas, practices, and influences. The creativity of all thinkers is analyzed by contextualizing their contributions from their respective historical locales. This chapter reviews their specific influence on education as well as civic movements both at home and abroad. It concludes by discussing issues related to global citizenship education for the twenty-first century, in particular, the contributions that a study of such thinkers can make in advancing our understanding of intercultural relations, issues of equity, and social justice. Further, such studies can enable readers to acquire critical understandings of the field of politics and complexities of political processes in contemporary societies.

The Educational and Political Creativity of Makiguchi, Ikeda, and Gandhi

Makiguchi and Gandhi were contemporaries who functioned in two different national contexts. Whereas in the early twentieth century, Japan was colonizing parts of South East Asia, India was a colony of the British Empire. Both Makiguchi and Gandhi confronted the authoritarianism in different countries—which for Makiguchi was the imperialism and nationalism of the Japanese government and for Gandhi was the racism in South Africa and the British Raj in India. However, there was a difference in the nature of the authoritarians they each confronted, and this was one of the reasons why these two contemporaries experienced a dissimilar fate. Whereas Makiguchi was imprisoned by the dictatorial Japanese government for his statements denouncing the emperor and the war, Gandhi, on the other hand, was dealing with the colonizer within the movement for Indian independence and was established as the political leader of the Indian National Congress. Further, Gandhi was able to extend his moral and political influence as the *bapu* or Father of the Nation while at the same time building a powerful political base.

Both Makiguchi and Gandhi aspired to transform their respective societies and education played an important role in this transformation. Makiguchi hoped to contribute to this transformation through his education and practice, whereas Gandhi was able to make a major political impact within Indian society through the *satyagraha* movement, or movement based on the force of "truth," and through the use of media to disseminate his ideas.[3] Common to both thinkers was the normative aspect of their ideas, their reliance on "truth" as the law of the universe and their perception of the interdependence of human life. Makiguchi's theory of education known as the value-creating theory and Gandhi's political philosophy at the individual level aimed to make citizens more socially responsible.

Makiguchi and the Origins of Soka Education Pedagogy

Makiguchi was born on June 6, 1871 (Fig. 2.1). The last decade of the nineteenth century witnessed the transformation of the Japanese society "from a feudal, largely agrarian society into a modern industrial power (that) was accompanied by large-scale dislocation and disruption" (Ikeda 2001: 2–3). Within his lifetime Japan went through an intense change from liberalism to fundamentalism. By the end of the nineteenth century, Japan had opened its doors to Europe and America and rather quickly succeeded in catching up with Western countries in terms of industry, science, and technology. However, in the succeeding Meiji (1868–1912) and Taisho (1912–1926) period, Japanese nationalism heightened under the monarchy and even further during the Second World War (1939–1945).

His personal circumstances were difficult because he was abandoned by his parents and brought up by relatives who were even unable to afford to send him to school. However, in spite of his adversities, Makiguchi trained as a teacher in the early part of the twentieth century and subsequently developed his own educational pedagogy through his 30 years of classroom teaching and perusing books by Japanese and Western authors. As Goulah and Gebert (2009) note, "His writings on education covered three main areas, human geography, community studies, and value-creating pedagogy" (ibid.: 115).

His educational pedagogy, *Soka kyoikugaku taikei* (The System of Value-Creating Education), is a pragmatic theory of knowledge and had implications for revitalizing teaching and learning processes and impact the education system as a whole. The key term in Makiguchi's pedagogy is *soka* (創価) or value creation, a neology formed from the two words, *so* from *sozo* (創造) or creation and *ka* from *kachi* (価値) or value. "Value creation" has the purpose of enhancing human life that can be nurtured by the educational process. As Bethel explains, for Makiguchi,

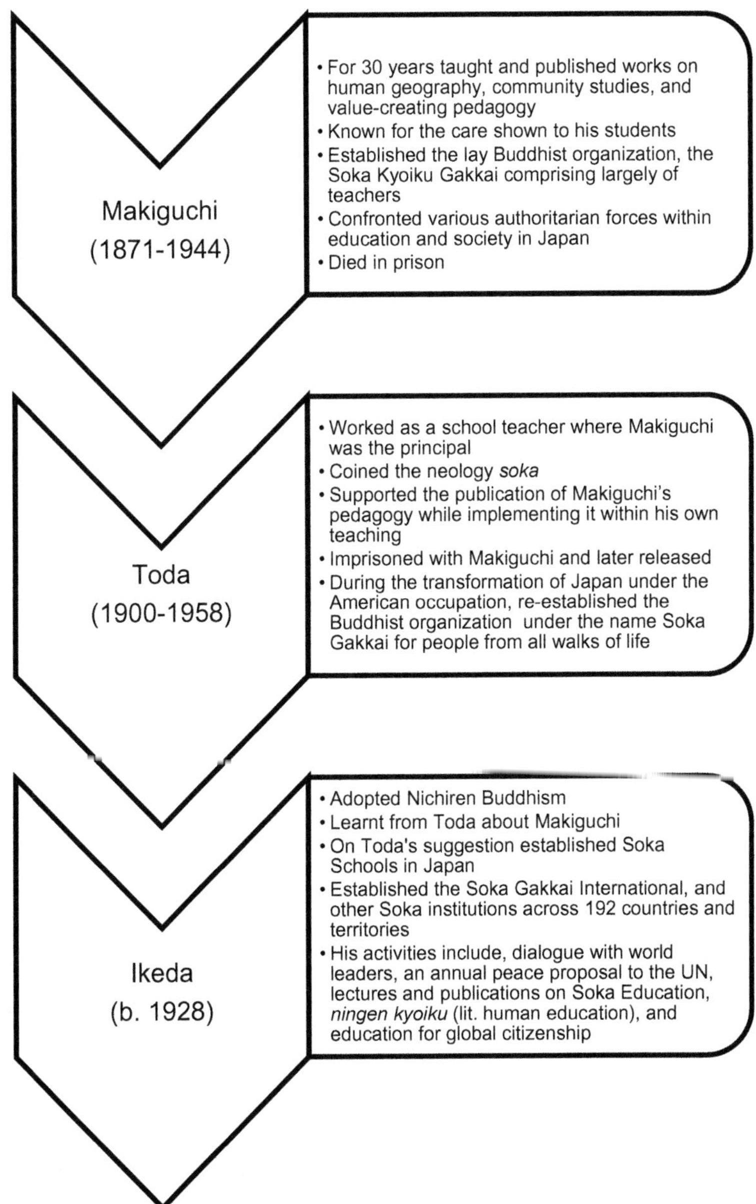

Fig. 2.1 A brief introduction to the progenitors of *soka*

"soka" formed a key word and a key concept, "Creation of value is part and parcel of what it means to be a human being. Human beings do not have the ability to create material; but they can create value, and it is in the creation of value that the unique meaning of human life lies" (Bethel 1973: 49).

To explain further, according to Makiguchi, the aim of education was to be derived from the aim of life. In his opinion, everyone ultimately desires to lead a happy life, and so the aim of education should be the happiness of the individual. According to his value-creating pedagogy, individual happiness is a state in which one lives "contributively," that is, through creating value for individual benefit as well as the good of society. Addressing this key concern Makiguchi states:

> Education consists of finding value within the living environment, thereby discovering physical and psychological principles that govern our lives and eventually applying these newfound principles in real life to create new value. In sum, it is the guided acquisition of skills of observation, comprehension, and application.
>
> (Bethel 1989: 168)

Makiguchi's pedagogy is a pragmatic theory of knowledge and has implications for revitalizing teaching and learning processes. As a teacher, Makiguchi carried out research which was conducted through "the scientist's method of inducting findings from actual experience" (Bethel 1989: 8) despite the fact that the trend which educationalists followed was to imitate foreign theories at home. Makiguchi faced the disadvantage in not being a highly qualified academic, but "only a school teacher." Social acceptance of his educational work was important to Makiguchi, and he spared no efforts to form relations with eminent people in politics and education, such as Tsuyoshi Inukai, the Prime Minister of Japan from December 1931 to May 1932; Magoichi Tsuwara, minister of commerce and industry; and Itamu Takagi, professor of medicine at Tokyo Imperial University. Arguably, for Makiguchi the role of an educator was to extend the boundaries beyond the classroom, and he himself wanted his work to have an impact on the Japanese education system as a whole.

In addition, Makiguchi's adversities during his childhood became the source of his deep compassion for the children he taught as a school teacher and principal. For example, he would always have some hot water ready in which to gently soak the children's hands, he would buy stationary at reduced prices from wholesalers for his students, and use his personal resources to prepare lunch for the children whose parents could not afford it. Due to the continued efforts of Makiguchi and a young teacher in his school, Josei Toda (1900–1958), the number of juvenile delinquents, as well as children with skin diseases considerably reduced in the school.

In the latter years of his educational career, Makiguchi realized that education in schools, without the necessary societal and structural change, was not adequate to actualize his proposals for value-creating education (see Sharma 2008). For instance, his proposal of "half day learning" at school and part of the day as an apprentice was not readily accepted within the educational structure and system of the modernizing and industrializing Meiji era (1868–1912). In the later years, the militaristic government indoctrinated the youth to participate in the war and this was also something that Makiguchi could not accept.

In 1928, Makiguchi became a Buddhist and formed a Buddhist educators group called the Soka Kyoiku Gakkai (Value-Creating Education Society). Whereas some critics, such as Brannen (1964) and Bethel (1973) claim that Makiguchi turned to religion as a solace and therefore established this society, it can be argued that Makiguchi formed this organization as a result of his understanding that a societal change was necessary for an educational transformation. This organization drew educators as well as other members of society who were interested in his value-creating theory as well as Nichiren Buddhism. Makiguchi's speeches to this group were not only to do with education, but also religion, society, and politics. Makiguchi was imprisoned because of his statements denouncing the emperor and the Japanese war. Unfortunately, unlike Gandhi, Makiguchi was unable to influence the Japanese people politically and generate an impact within the political processes of the Japanese society. Also, apart from his colleague Toda, who even went to prison with Makiguchi, there was no active and political support from the Japanese people for Makiguchi, including a lack of support from the Soka Kyoiku Gakkai for his release. Subsequently, Makiguchi died as a prisoner on November 18, 1944.

Today, in the twenty-first century, Makiguchi is not well known within the political or educational circles of Japan. As Kumagai states, he is not even mentioned in the 1971 "Modern Educational History of Japan Dictionary," which attests to the fact that although several scholars and eminent persons during Makiguchi's time admired his work, just forty years after the publication of his educational pedagogy he was virtually unknown in the educational circles of modern Japan (Kumagai 2000). In a previous study that argued for the need to engage with Makiguchi's work for present day education, I had examined the following lines of thought as being central to his work: the relation between the learner's geographical environment and the process of value creation; the view of happiness of the individual as an aim of value-creating education; the recognition of the sociological dimensions of education for value creation; a pragmatic education—creating value through the use of experience and scientific method; and relative value in education and absolute value of religious experience (Sharma 2008: 53–61). Some of these core ideas will be revisited in the following chapters.

Numerous reasons can be stated for the continued lack of knowledge of Makiguchi and his values in Japan. At the educational level Harima (1997) points out that chief among the main factors that have deterred the application of Makiguchi's ideas even today is the tendency within the Japanese educators to be easily influenced by foreigners even at the cost of overlooking the ideas of Japanese thinkers.

The lack of initiative to understand and challenge political and economic machines can be another reason why the general public has not seriously engaged with the Soka Gakkai, or its leader Makiguchi. The Soka Gakkai is the successor to the organization Soka Kyoiku Gakkai which was established by Makiguchi in 1930. It presently includes roughly one tenth of Japan's population, and now does have a political view since it provides political endorsement to the Komeito party (Clean Government Party; literally: Justice Party), that was launched in 1964, and has been part of the ruling coalition with the Liberal Democratic Party (LDP) since 1999 (excluding 2009–2011). As a growing political entity, it has been of interest to both the Japanese politicians and the media. Watanabe's research concludes that the latter has gone on to generate a wrong image of the *gakkai* in Japanese society, through "distortions generated in the reportage of the Soka Gakkai"[4] (Watanabe 2000: 213).

Notwithstanding this, Makiguchi's ideas have gained popularity in some parts of Japan and abroad in spite of the fact that during his lifetime the practical application of his value-creating theory had taken place mainly within his own classrooms and in Toda's *Jishu Gakkan* educational institution. However, due to the post-war reconstruction of the Soka Gakkai by Toda, and his successor the current honorary President,

Ikeda, Makiguchi is now known to the Soka Gakkai members in 192 countries, and research (by members and non-members) is being carried out on his educational ideas. It should be mentioned here that outside Japan, Soka Gakkai International (SGI) organizations do not engage in politics. The SGI is also registered as a non-governmental organization (NGO) with formal ties to the United Nations (UN), and Ikeda submits a peace proposal every year to the UN as a Buddhist outlining his views and suggestions on current and relevant global issues.

Ikeda and Education for Global Citizenship

Born on January 2, 1928 in Tokyo, Ikeda witnessed the brutal consequences of a nation at war and the personal tragedies it brings to the ordinary people, including the death of his one brother in Burma, and three others who too were drafted. Although from humble beginnings as the son of seaweed farmers, Ikeda shares fond memories of his home and local community. In spite of a weak physical constitution, compounded by tuberculosis, the young Daisaku was an avid reader of books and literature from all over the world. Searching for the meaning of life in war-torn Japan, Ikeda met Toda in 1947 at a Buddhist meeting where he was taken to by a friend. Toda became his mentor for the rest of his life, as he studied with him, worked for his business, and eventually succeeded him as the third president of the Soka Gakkai lay Buddhist organization in 1960. Since then Ikeda has invested himself in peace, culture, and education related activities within home and abroad, including the establishment of 15 Soka kindergartens, primary and secondary schools, women's college, and universities in seven countries across Asia and the Americas.

Education for global citizenship is a key theme within Ikeda's educational ideas and proposals as will be discussed in Chapter 4. Here I would like to draw attention to terms that need further analysis through *soka*/Ikeda studies. For example, the term "planetary citizenship," which is the title of a dialogue between the futurist, Hazel Henderson, and Ikeda (2004); the term "cosmopolitan citizenship" that appears in a few scholarly work in this field (Miller 2002; Obelleiro 2012); and the use of "world citizenship," which has recently been argued as the closest translation to describe the intent within *soka* pedagogy and practice.[5] For the purpose and aims of this book, Ikeda's proposals for citizenship are contextualized within the discourse on global citizenship education that are both centered on the initiatives of the UN.

Also here it is important to reference the shift from Makiguchi's *Soka kyoikugaku taikei* (The System of Value-Creating Pedagogy) to Ikeda's *Soka kyoiku* or Soka Education (value-creating education). In relation to the current use of Makiguchi and Ikeda's ideas, one of the outcomes of an earlier study which concentrated on key documents of the Soka Schools in Japan revealed that, "there is a mixture of aims and values within these schools that stems from the national educational aims, as well as Makiguchi's value-creating pedagogy, along with which certain Buddhist ideals, that are all incorporated under the use of the term 'value-creating education' within the school documents" (Sharma 2008: 113). Chapter 1 also referred to Ikeda's use of the term "Soka education" or "Soka Education" to characterize the educational approach passed down from Makiguchi and Toda and practiced in the Soka schools that he has founded (Ikeda 2010 in Goulah and Ito 2012: 60–61).

Further, the term "Soka Education" (value-creating education) is the title of Ikeda's (2001) book that is a collection of his university addresses and proposals on education. At the same time, Ikeda largely uses the term *ningen kyoiku* (humanistic education) when expressing his views and aspiration for education in general. For instance, he proposes that education should aim at the students' happiness which is connected to their ability to live contributive lives and in creating value for the welfare of others, and that this goal can be realized through the nurturing relationship between the teacher and student (see Goulah 2010; Goulah and Gebert 2009; Ito 2005, 2007).

Based on my long-term observational studies, discussions with the teachers and staff, as well as content analysis of key documents of the Soka Schools established by Ikeda (Sharma 2008), two factors can be attributed to the successful application of Makiguchi and Ikeda's proposals in these schools. First, there is a willingness among the teachers to experiment with the value-creating theory of Makiguchi as well as Ikeda's educational ideas and proposals. Second, is Ikeda's initiative to bring recognition to Makiguchi and Toda's lives and work as the progenitors of *soka*. Toda serves as the link between Makiguchi and Ikeda because Ikeda joined the Soka Gakkai after Makiguchi's death. Bethel states that, "Ikeda, as Makiguchi, sees education as the most important factor in changing the present reality" (Bethel 1973: 121). Further, he adds that Ikeda and Makiguchi both laid emphasis on the "need for a harmonious balance within every person's life between the pursuit of values of personal gain and the pursuit of values of social good. One cannot, in other words, be a complete, happy, value-creating person by himself" (Bethel 1973: 121). This philosophy enthuses both teachers and students of the Soka Schools to be active participants in their local communities, as well as engaging in international exchanges.[6]

Makiguchi and Ikeda have both endeavored to contribute to the processes which could transform their respective societies in intellectual and moral terms through the use of religion and politics. As Bethel analyzes in his work *Makiguchi the value creator*,

> In Soka Gakkai, under Ikeda's leadership, intellect is not pressed into the service of the movement, but rather is aimed at transforming the quality of mind of the entire population, equipping that population to judge the movement and to hold both it and its competitors accountable...Soka Gakkai may well be breaking open new frontiers in this respect.
>
> (Bethel 1973: 143)

Bethel however, does not address the issue of how the Soka Gakkai in practical terms has achieved this transformation. For example, he does not engage with the structures and institutions that the progenitors of *soka* have established that engage with this task of social-self actualization. As argued earlier, Makiguchi must have established the Soka Kyoiku Gakkai because he realized that education on its own could not compensate for society, such as argued by Bernstein (1970: 345). One of the reasons that Makiguchi was unable to "succeed" as an educationalist was because he did not have the adequate institutional or societal support required for his proposals to be implemented (as pointed out earlier). In light of this Makiguchi's speeches within the *gakkai* on the existing socio-political events can be seen as his efforts to enable the members to become more politically aware. Similarly, today, Ikeda and the Soka Gakkai in Japan claim that their religion is not an "opiate," and have therefore engaged in influencing Japanese culture and politics through the various institutions established by Ikeda within Japan and abroad.[7]

Gandhi, Education, and Politics in Satyagraha

Gandhi's role as an educator extended beyond the schools within his *ashrams* or communities, to an engagement with the youth and polity at large as the leader of the millions and the *mahatma*. His educational role encompassed learning to use the *charkha* (spinning wheel), wearing handmade *khadi* cloth, protecting the cow from being slaughtered, and other economic and social reforms that were aimed at boycotting British goods as well as the liberation of the people. He also wanted to transform the minds of the Indians and educate the populace to a life of values that contributed to both the individual and social welfare. The Congress Party viewed this as an effective policy, but to Gandhi, who was born into Jainism and practiced Hinduism, it was his creed that stemmed from his commitment to *ahimsa* or non-violence. This he hoped would allow the Indians to see "the universal and all-pervading spirit of Truth leading to identification with everything that lives" (Gandhi 1957: 504). Unlike the Congress Party, Gandhi saw his movement as an educational one, in which the educator (himself in this case) was also a role model. Through his own experiments, Gandhi as the *bapu* (or father) hoped to lead people to understand and practice a life of truth and non-violence.

In fact, values, such as non-violence were able to generate an impact not only because it was pertinent, but due to the methods of application within the context of the Indian political movement. Gandhi was constantly creating values in his engagement with politics, religion, economics, industry, and education. In *satyagraha* the values of non-violence, tolerance, love for humanity, among others, were constantly associated with Gandhi's personality, his symbols, and the entire movement (as elaborated further on in this chapter).

Dalton borrows from Burns to attribute to Gandhi the role of an educator, and states,

> Burns gives to the conception of leadership a normative dimension that Plato stressed but that is often missing in contemporary political science analysis. Burns views the leader as essentially an educator engaged in a creative relationship with followers. Gandhi saw Satyagraha as heuristic because it employed a kind of power that encouraged reflection and reexamination of motives, needs, and interests. He believed, as Burns suggests, that this educative procedure depended on the development of an engagement of all those involved in a situation to extend awareness of human needs and the means of gratifying them.
>
> (Dalton 1993: 193)

Within each act of the *satyagraha* was Gandhi's aim of transforming himself as the leader and those he led, in order to move his people and their country further on the path of independence or *swaraj*.

Another vital purpose of Gandhi's education, as Dalton notes, was "that satyagraha must be used to gain the empowerment of those who had never been politicized" (ibid.: 194).

However, this two-pronged educational approach—the liberation of the individual and the independence of the country—was difficult to sustain due to several factors, such as the ideological differences between Gandhi and the Congress political party and its leader Nehru who was a protégé of Gandhi; the regular eruption of violence within the Indian independence movement that interrupted its progress; and the contradictions that surrounded Gandhi while he tried to bring together diverse groups of people and communities with vested interests in a multicultural Indian society.

Gandhi had to use political creativity to bring the numerous sections of the Indian community to work together toward the common goal of social transformation and national independence. Let us engage here with Gandhi's intercultural understandings and ingenuity.

Intercultural aspects of Gandhi's own life are an important factor in his attempts to deal with "the other" through dialogue. His Indian, Gujarati, Hindu background and diasporic experiences in England and South Africa have particular relevance to the socially diverse polity of present-day democratic nation states. This is especially relevant because it is indicative of the various layers of identities of the diaspora which influenced his understandings of particularities. As a person embodying ideas of "Indian-ness" these excluded notions of the caste and the *jati*.

The first phase of his intercultural experiences was not only unusual but perhaps more radical than other Indians during his time. Born in Porbandar, in the West part of India, on October 2, 1869, Gandhi's departure for England at the age of 19 despite the religious strictures of crossing the *kala pani* or "black waters," was an indication of his radical departure from austere cultural norms. He describes his father, who was the chief minister of Porbandar as "a lover of his clan, truthful, brave and generous" (Gandhi 1982: 19). Referring to his mother, Putlibai, he states,

> The outstanding impression my mother has left on my memory is that of saintliness. She was deeply religious. She would not think of taking her meals without her daily prayers...She would take the hardest vows and keep them without flinching. Illness was no excuse for relaxing them.
>
> (ibid.: 20)

He came from a strict *modh bania* (trader) caste. His arrival in London and the metropolis and adoption of dress and manners paradoxically strengthened his notions of identification with the British Raj (or rule). The adoption of vegetarianism and study of classic Indian texts in English translation were part of a self-conscious understanding of himself. His acquisition of a legal qualification before his return to India not only equipped him as a professional lawyer but also sharpened his understanding of the ambiguities and anomalies in the field of law.

The second phase of his intercultural experiences started with his departure to South Africa and his understandings were informed by the repertoires of experiences in these diasporic contexts. He had to negotiate within himself not only the complex set of identities but also of experiences. In 1893, as a professional and shy commercial lawyer, his exposure to brutal colonial racism in South Africa was very different from his diasporic student experiences in London. It provided a further deepening of his intellectual and spiritual journeys. While remaining a loyal subject of the Empire and its constitutional framework, his sympathies lay with the Boers in South Africa. He also made some political inroads with a campaign against the electoral suppression of the franchise for rich Natal Indian merchants in 1894. He used political activities, such as distributing pamphlets, and the passing of moderate resolutions using legal arguments.

The commitment to the Indian cause in South Africa was further developed after his return there in 1902, the setting up of the Indian Opinion, a weekly paper in Durban, and the establishment of Phoenix Farm in 1904. Further, the 1906 Transvaal Asiatic Amendment Act to finger print all Indians led to the political campaigning for all Indians, not just the merchants. It was during this phase of twenty-one years that his activism became manifest and a commitment to the community and public life matured. In particular, as Claude Markovits writes:

> Between 1907 and 1913 he gradually perfected a technique of political agitation which he called *satyagraha* to distinguish it from 'passive resistance' with which it is generally equated.
>
> (Markovits 2003: 4)

The development of *satyagraha* as an active political resistance using non-violent methods, and the writing of the book, *Hind Swaraj* or Indian Home Rule in 1909 was not only a critique of Western civilization but also an elaboration of his political philosophy. The deepening of these ideas was marked by the October 1913 miners march from Natal to Transvaal and it pre-figures the 1930 Salt March in India (Swan 1985, also see Fischer 1982, Hardiman 2003, and Parekh 1995).[8] At a meeting in Durban in 1913 to mourn the Indian miners killed he was moved to wearing an Indian attire, *lungi* and *kurta* for the first time. The South African experience therefore forms the basis of re-inventing tradition which he subsequently used to great effect in India. It seems to be a direct result of the relationship between the struggle of the subordinated South African Indian community and the longer term development by Gandhi of his own political practice.

His return to India in 1915 was the beginning of the third phase of the maturation of his political ideas which allowed the cumulative understandings in all the previous contexts to be used to connect with the Indian masses. However, his understandings derived from the 300,000 oppressed Indian minority of different castes and religions in South Africa was qualitatively and quantitatively different from the diversity of 300 million Indians. In order to establish himself in India, he started to build a political base in the western state of Gujarat as well as making a linguistic shift from English to Hindustani and Gujarati. These shifts in political experiences accompanied by linguistic shifts also meant that Gandhi was developing a political and lexical vocabulary which would be suitable for the Indian freedom struggle.

Here it can be argued that Gandhi's understanding of politics was not a purely Western one, but had strong indigenous elements. The new political vocabulary he used constitutes terms that cannot be comprehended within a Western understanding of politics. Gandhi's political culture was based on the concept of law that was understood by the Indian polity. Whereas he used his skills as a civil lawyer as stated earlier, to write petitions and so on, he was also invoking the "common brotherhood" of the disparate but intercultural Indian community through appealing to their shared understanding of a "causal law," that is even now expressed in popular terms, such as fate, destiny, or the will of God (Bhagvan or Allah). Thereby Gandhi's political culture made use of both the notion of law that had come in from the West but also created an indigenous political theory that took the causal law or *satya* as a peg, to which were added terms borrowed from the diverse communities, such as *ahimsa* from Jainism, *dharma* from Hinduism, love from Christianity, and notions of equality from the Buddhist *sangha*.

The appeal this made to the popular culture was the greatest asset for Gandhi's movement. But this can be misunderstood if we do not examine the persona of Gandhi. There can be said to be two Gandhis. The first is Gandhi the person, for whom truth and non-violence was his creed. Then there was the Gandhi who had to play the role of the *mahatma*, the moral leader and a nationalist, who had to work through the problematic intercultural issues.

In London's Tavistock Square stands a statue of Mahatma Gandhi. It is exactly opposite the site of the 7/7 bus bombing. In a professorial address delivered at the Institute of Education next door, two years before this incident Gundara (2003) had mentioned:

> It is a matter of fundamental importance that the role of religion in multi-faith, constitutional and democratic states is clearly defined to avoid these states being lead to a brink of fundamentalist and dogmatic notions of 'truth' fuelled by faith.
>
> The importance of Gandhi and his protégé Nehru in the present context is that they had a genuine intercultural understanding of Western and Indian civilizations. They personified a creativity and determination which is currently lacking in many political and educational leaders.
>
> (Gundara 2003: 12–13)

Unlike the bombers, Gandhi's notion of "truth" was not exclusive or fuelled by a desire to cause destruction to the "others." Gandhi's creativity was certainly an outcome of his intercultural understandings of the different concepts of "truth" (as stated above), which stands as a polar opposite to the narrowest definition of "truth" held by the London July bombers. It must be added that this is the same concern that underlined Makiguchi's declaration in the early part of the twentieth century that, in the spectrum of "values" there is no need for a separate sanctity or sacred value as expressed by Western thinkers like Winderband (see Bethel 1989: 84). Instead, he advocated the "value of good" that he found exists in our creative contribution to society's welfare through our actions for protecting human dignity and the sanctity of life.

After 1920, Gandhi had begun to intensify his identity as a nationalist. He had begun to think that the liberation of the Indian people would also lead to the liberation of the British people and hence the development of his struggles was directed at the imperium and not at individuals. He then started in earnest to develop interventions in Champaran in Bihar, an involvement in the Ahmedabad strike, and these interventions were sharpened by the Rowlatt Bills which suppressed political dissent.

The experience of the jail and the turn toward social reform by focusing on untouchability, the promotion of the *khadi* cloth, as well as the role of education, the carefully designed curriculum within his *ashrams*, and the consequent proposals for *Nai Talim* (lit. "new education," also known as the Wardha Scheme of Education), and Constructive Program are further markers in his intercultural journey (Sharma 1999: 31–34; Sharma 2008, Chapter 4). The focus on his attire was based on the deliberate process of self-definition and identity construction. He used contemporary media as well as political party apparatus to mobilize the ordinary masses including the peasants (Green 1993).

His intercultural understandings are evidenced by his attempts to bring equalities within the Hindu community by eradicating caste differences, the attempts to reconcile the differences between Hindu and Muslim communities and at the political organization level by reconciling the Congress Party and the Muslim League. His opposition to the caste system did not arise because he was a Hindu but because he was a reformer and as Nandy suggests, "a modern Indian nationalist" (Nandy 1983: 48).

The partition of India at the time of its independence in 1947 for very complex reasons was a deep blow to Gandhi because he had continued to think that religious differences were superficial and that his version of Indian nationalism could accommodate these differences. He nevertheless, continued to wade into areas of religious violence and retained his moral high ground in politics. From 1937 onwards, his name was mentioned for the Nobel Peace Prize but "the Eurocentrism of the Norwegian Committee deprived him of an award many thought he deserved" (Markovits 2003: 22–23).

On January 31, 1948, Gandhi was assassinated by a Hindu radical. Making Gandhi the "Father of the Nation" turned him into an icon as the "founding father of secular nationalism," which Nehru, as the first Prime Minister of independent India, sought to promote as the ideology of the new republic.

The Impact on Civic Movements

Gandhi's Lineage: Within India and Abroad

A critique of Gandhi's work has also developed both within India as well as internationally. The Marxists and communists ideologically and organizationally opposed Gandhi's ideas as did the narrow Indian nationalists.

However, there have also been others who have supported Gandhi's work that have included Vinoba Bhave, the Bhoodan Movement, the work of socialist Ram Manohar Lohia and Jayaprakash Narayan, who called for a "Total Revolution" and subsequently became part of the Janata Coalition, led by Morarji Desai which ironically defeated the Congress Party (which Gandhi founded) in 1977 thirty years after Gandhi's death and invoked Gandhism as an ideology of the Indian state.

In the bi-polar context at the international level Gandhi's ideas were used from micro-level struggles against poverty as well to liberate the poor in Mafia-bound Sicily by Danilo Dolci in 1952 in Italy, and in 1953 by Lanza del Vasto who used a Gandhi-like fast to protest against the French war in Algeria. Gandhi's principles have also been used by the anti-globalization activist Jose Bove (who was imprisoned in France for burning a McDonald's), and Ernest Schumacher in his 1973 book *Small is beautiful* incorporated Gandhi's ideas on the development of village industries. Gandhi's inspiration was also acknowledged by the Brundtland Commission in 1987. The environmentalists in India like the *chipko* movement and Petra Kelly of the Green Party in Germany also subscribed to his ideas and inspiration. Whether the numerous movements which have arisen are based on his thought and action or on his position as an icon is an open question.

In sharp contrast to the political successors of Gandhi (like Martin Luther King who appeared on the international stage soon after Gandhi's passing away), within India the use of Gandhi and his ideas has been mostly contextual. Terms, such as Gandhian and Gandhism have continued to be used extensively by various sections of the Indian society—academia, politics, media, civil servants, and the general public. References to these concepts have often suited the context of those who speak of Gandhi—in speeches made at public gatherings or in printed material for the readership of the educated few. Though there have been some practitioners of Gandhi's views, in general one finds that Gandhi is more often than not used by those in positions of power to suit their own end (see Sharma 2008: 95–96). In essence, whereas some scholars contend that Gandhi is still relevant in modern India, critics find him as merely a picture hanging on the walls of government, police, and court buildings. One of the forums that can meaningfully re-engage with Gandhi and global citizenship is the UNESCO Mahatma Gandhi Institute of Education for Peace and

Sustainable Development (MGIEP) set up in New Delhi. The Institute engages with important peace and sustainability issues with particular focus on the Asia-Pacific region. There is however, no real engagement here as yet with Gandhi or his ideas.

Expanding the Network of Soka Through Dialogue

In contrast however, Makiguchi's history within his own lifetime and after his death has been very different from Gandhi. In his own lifetime, Makiguchi did not face the challenges that Gandhi had to confront as a national leader. However, Makiguchi had demonstrated great courage by standing up against the educational, political, and religious authoritarian establishments of his society. As a school teacher and principal, he refused to curry favor with the children of influential parents and therefore was made to transfer from one school to another until he was forced to retire in 1929. Later on, as a Buddhist leader, Makiguchi openly voiced his concerns for the equality and dignity of life, denouncing the emperor as a common man. His actions angered the religious and political authorities of his time for which he faced imprisonment and subsequent death. His predicament as a teacher in Japan has ramifications for many millions of teachers in authoritarian states at the present time who suffer a range of privations. This adds to the denial of teaching and learning of millions of young people in many non-democratic states.

Makiguchi's successor Ikeda can be likened to Gandhi in his engagement with the social and political transformation of his country. Fisker-Nielsen's (2012) research shows that in recent years the Komeito party has become well known for implementing varied welfare policies in Japan, as well as, it has been a major force in the normalization of Japan–China relations in the early 1970s under Ikeda's influence. Also, as an outcome, this study reveals some of the complex challenges that have confronted this party, the *gakkai* movement, and other groups within the Japanese polity, particularly in the aftermath of 9/11. Although the issue is quite complex, to explain briefly, article 9 of the Japanese Constitution prohibits Japan from engaging in the threat or use of force except for the purpose of its own self-defense. The Self-Defense Forces (SDF), established in 1954 enabled Japan to focus on economic development while it outsourced its defense needs to the United States. However, more recently, Japan was drawn to defend its allies, for example, the US-led war on Iraq in March 2003. Such political realities have been confronted through anti-war protests by several groups, including the Soka Gakkai, who advocate for peace through peaceful means. As a response, the Komeito has imposed limitations on Japan's military through legislations, although, as Fisker-Nielsen suggests, "the LDP had not wanted any limits on the logistical aid that Japan's Self-Defense Forces (SDF) could provide to its security partners" (Fisker-Nielsen 2016: 2).

The examples of the Soka Gakkai and Komeito in Japan, and Gandhi's political movement in India, show the complexities in the use of "values," such as peace and non-violence, within the reality of politics. At the same time, this critical appraisal does not attempt to overlook the necessity and importance of the citizen's engagement in political transformation and the role played by the Soka Gakkai in endorsing public accountability from the governing political power (see Held 1987: 267–268).

In particular, the powerful use of Makiguchi's concept of *soka* or value creation by Ikeda within the realm of Japanese society and politics has provided an example of the positive use of religious values in a public domain. It has shown that personal values can be of benefit not only to the individual but also to the society at large, as long as the use of values is educationally oriented with a focus on the political education of the members who in turn hold the political powers accountable.

Further, as an individual citizen Ikeda has taken action to initiate dialogue with people and countries including China, the Soviet Union, and Cuba in spite of the hostility toward these nations during that time. This he states was "despite criticism" based on his "stance as a Buddhist" and his "citizen's diplomacy" (Ikeda 1999: 129–130). A similar level of detail as devoted to my study of Gandhi's politics and Fisker-Nielson's (2012, 2016) examination of the Soka Gakkai's civil society role in Japan, needs to be done on Ikeda and the Soka Gakkai. For example, a study of Soka as a socio-cultural-educational movement of engaged citizens across 192 countries that practice similar core beliefs while dialoging with particularities.

The Relevance of a Study of *Satyagraha* and *Soka* to Global Citizenship Education

In relation to the above discussions, the underlying concern of this chapter has been with global citizenship and political education. The exposition of Makiguchi, Gandhi and Ikeda's political understandings were studied in relation to their place as citizens of their respective countries.

Further, there have been civic movements in their respective countries and abroad to which their contribution can be delineated in certain ways.

The ideas and practices of these thinkers for a field of study and practice carry considerable educational weight in the twenty-first century. Global citizenship education somehow occupies the paradoxical position of being recognized generally as of central importance while being treated as peripheral in many educational institutions. There is, in effect, a struggle in process over the "values" which should inform the development of global citizenship education, especially in democratic societies.

Global citizenship education has been a topic of concern for education in many modern nation states as discussed in more detail in the next chapter. In this new century of global terrorism and Islamophobia, living with the "other" is an issue that urgently needs to be addressed. *Learning to live together* is an initiative of UNESCO that was originally forwarded by the Delors Commission in 1996, and has greater currency after 9/11. The commission highlights six major paradoxes of globalization and the challenges of education for living together. Compared to this initiative by UNESCO, the conference on *Learning to live together* which took place in 1936 in Utrecht was centered on the need for morality underpinned by religious "values," in an age in which industrial and scientific development had begun to raise concerns about the breakdown of communities and values (Rawson 1936).

However, there are also political implications of *learning to live together* which we need to consider as discussed further in this book. For example, the task of educating students to understand the contextual use of values which may be politicized or de-politicized. Today in India many "Gandhians" writ large have de-politicized Gandhi and his values. This *re-appearance* of Gandhi in a way very different from his intentions is an example of the argument that Herbert Marcuse makes on the classics of literature, philosophy, and politics which, in becoming available in paperbacks in local bookstore

> have left the mausoleum to come to life again...but coming to life as classics, they come to life as other than themselves; they are deprived of their antagonistic force, of the estrangement which was the very condition of their truth. The intent and function of these works have thus fundamentally changed. If they once stood out in contradiction to the status quo, this contradiction is now flattened out.
>
> (Marcuse 1972: 24)

Expounding on Marcuse's argument, Ferguson states, "One of the consequences of Marcuse's analysis is, he suggests, that if one tries to conceptualize the world differently, one's arguments will not be accepted as valid for consideration until they have been reduced to the terms of the existing universe of discourse" (Ferguson 1998: 25). Though there is an extremity in the analysis Marcuse makes of the closing of the universe of discourse, his claims cannot be completely dismissed. It has been seen through this study on the presence of Gandhi that though he continues to be invoked, his writings do not make the significant contribution they did within his own time. As noted earlier, Gandhi's ideas and values engaged various colonial governments in many different ways, such as through his role as the political leader of the Indian National Congress, his moral influence and perceived image as the Father of the Nation, and the impact of his movement of *satyagraha* especially after the Salt March of 1930, all of which are now framed within the Indian history textbooks.

At the same time, though there has been a "de-politicization" of Gandhi, there has been an opposite change in the case of Makiguchi. Whereas both Gandhi and Makiguchi had opposed their respective governments, Gandhi was an activist who was seen as a growing threat by a politically astute British colonial administrator. While Makiguchi was an educator who was perceived as an annoyance by the autocratic leaders of his own Japanese government, as was the Nichiren (Buddhist) temple, and the school authorities in which he taught and served as principal.

Therefore, it is argued here that in spite of the leading discourse, or "socially constructed knowledge" (Kress and Leeuwen 2001) that exists within societies, that have been formed largely by the agendas of power-holders there are new discourses that arise constantly to challenge the existing ones. On the one hand, dissident thinkers like Gandhi are made "safe" in India by depriving them of their oppositional political force, while others like Makiguchi in Japan have assumed such a political role after their death.

To bring out the sharp contrast in comparative terms between Gandhi's political influences during his own time as compared to Makiguchi's political impact after his death, this chapter has concentrated on Gandhi's engagement with the politics of his own time and the Soka Gakkai's growth after the founder's death. A vital implication of the above two examples of the politicization and de-politicization of thinkers like Makiguchi and Gandhi is that the ideas and values of dissident thinkers tend to lose their creativity and efficacy when they are used in a way that does not contend with the existing power structures of society. Values, such as non-violence, peace, and value creation to strengthen human rights are often processual, and can therefore be invoked, politicized, and de-politicized according to the context in which they are placed.

Conclusion and Moving Forward

To summarize, the focus of this chapter is educational, political, and comparative. This study engages with Makiguchi, Ikeda, and Gandhi's core ideas, creative strategies, behaviors, and beliefs as active protagonists in their respective countries. It reflects on how all three thinkers were motivated to take positive action based on their ideas and values. However, their fates have been dissimilar. Whereas Gandhi has no significant impact in India today as he did within his own time, in Japan and worldwide there is a growing influence of Makiguchi and Ikeda. Among the factors that determine their impact are whether or not their ideas have been used creatively and directly confront educational challenges and political processes.

Enhancing creativity and the courage to take bold collective efforts are lessons from this study for global citizenship education and its goal of *learning to live together* in the twenty-first century. As our future citizens, young people need to acquire such skills and sensibilities, toward which, as the next chapter argues, learning with the curriculum should represent diverse knowledge and wisdom from across human societies. At a basic level students can start with a rigorous study of the "values based politics" of Edmund Burke, Karl Marx, Gandhi, Ikeda, Mandela, and many others.

Notes

1. As an example within the Chinese context, as Professor Pei-I Chou at the National Sun Yat-sen University in Taiwan mentioned to me in a recent email, "Global Citizenship Education (GCE) is very much in its infancy in Eastern society and education until now, even though it can be traced back to some trends of ancient Chinese philosophy. The interpretations of GCE differ in different social systems and cultural traditions. For example, the definitions of human rights might differ in the perspectives of Protestantism and Confucianism. Most of the literature about Eastern perspectives within GCE that I know of are in Chinese" (Pei-I Chou, personal communication, July 6, 2017).

2. An engagement with the educational and political creativity of Makiguchi and Gandhi was the topic of consideration of a previous co-authored work with Prof. Jagdish Gundara (2008). The journal is presently out of circulation.
3. The word *satyagraha* comprises of the two words, *satya* (truth) and *agraha* (insistence or holding firmly to) which put together can be translated as non-violent resistance; a relentless search for truth; truth-force; holding on to truth. It is the term Gandhi used to describe the political movement lead by him for India's independence from the British Raj (or rule).
4. Among others, the Japanese media has tried to emphasize the Soka Gakkai's vast financial resources, and political power. Such as, articles suggesting that money is coaxed or coerced out of members. Other articles stir up suspicion against the Soka Gakkai and its political links with the Komeito political party. There has however been no evidence to suggest that the Soka Gakkai has gained in any direct way through the political endorsement it provides to the Komeito party. Further, as Watanabe's research shows, the speculative and baseless reports by the Japanese media have often been the result of the control exercised by "competing religious and political groups" (Watanabe 2000: 225). Watanabe's research shows that the "...matrix of influence and interests binding the media, state, and religion in Japan has impeded, within the Japanese press, the recognition that freedom of speech is the freedom to question and criticise those in the highest authority" (ibid.: 212). Watanabe argues that the "media coverage on *the reality of the activities* of the Soka Gakkai, Japan's largest religious organisation with an estimated membership of 4 million households, is virtually nonexistent" (ibid., emphasis added). Instead, the Japanese press and Jiminto or Liberal Democratic Party (LDP) officials have tried to falsely represent the Soka Gakkai as a religious organization that aims to eventually "take over Japan and impose its belief as a state religion" through its increasing financial and political strengths (ibid.: 218).
5. Jason Goulah notes the shift in the use of key terms related to the notion of global citizenship within Makiguchi, Toda, and Ikeda's work. For example, in 1903 Makiguchi uses the word *sekaimin* or "world people," in 1952 Toda mentions the term *chikyū minzoku shugi* that can be translated as "global race-ism/global people-ism/global ethnos-ism/or global nationalism"; in 1960 Ikeda uses the same term as Toda; in 1996 Ikeda refers to *chikyū shimin kyōiku* or "global citizenship education"; and in 1987 and 2014 Ikeda uses the phrase *sekai shimin kyōiku* or "world citizenship education," which Goulah finds to be closest to Ikeda's intension and views on education that comes through a study of his work (My notes from J. Goulah's panel presentation titled, Education for global citizenship, delivered at the *World Summit of Educators*, Soka University of America, California on June 12, 2016.).

6. See the activities by the Kansai Soka Schools at http://www.kansai.soka.ed.jp/.
7. For further details see: http://www.daisakuikeda.org/.
8. In March 1930, Gandhi and the other *satyagrahis* marched to the ocean to gather salt in a campaign to boycott the British.

References

Alston, L. (1910). *Education and citizenship in India*. London: Longmans.

Bernstein, B. (1970). Education cannot compensate for society. *New Society, 387*, 344–347.

Bethel, D. M. (1973). *Makiguchi the value creator: Revolutionary Japanese educator and founder of Soka Gakkai*. Tokyo: Weatherhill.

Bethel, D. M. (Ed.). (1989). *Education for creative living: Ideas and proposals of Tsunesaburo Makiguchi*. Ames: Iowa State University Press.

Brannen, N. S. (1964, June). Soka Gakkai's theory of value. *Contemporary Religions Japan, 5*, 143–154.

Dalton, D. (1993). *Mahatma Gandhi: Nonviolent power in action*. New York: Columbia University Press.

Delors, J., et al. (1996). *Learning: The treasure within*. Paris: UNESCO.

Ferguson, R. (1998). *Representing race: Ideology, identity and the media*. London: Arnold.

Fischer, L. (1982). *The life of Mahatma Gandhi*. St. Albans: Granada.

Fisker-Nielsen, A. M. (2012). *Religion and politics in contemporary Japan: Soka Gakkai youth and Komeito*. Japan Anthropology Workshop Series. London: Routledge.

Fisker-Nielsen, A. M. (2016). Has Komeito abandoned its principles? Public perception of the party's role in Japan's security legislation debate. *The Asia-Pacific Journal, 14*(21/3), 1–28.

Gandhi, M. K. (1957). *An autobiography or the story of my experiments with truth*. Boston: Beacon Press.

Gandhi, M. K. (1982). *An autobiography or the story of my experiments with truth*. London: Penguin Books.

Goulah, J. (2010). From (harmonious) community life to (creative) coexistence. Considering Daisaku Ikeda's educational philosophy in the Parker, Dewey, Makiguchi and Ikeda "reunion". *Schools: Studies Education, 7*(2), 253–275.

Goulah, J., & Gebert, A. (2009). Tsunesaburo Makiguchi: Introduction to the man, his ideas, and the special issue. *Educational Studies, 45*, 115–132.

Goulah, J., & Ito, T. (2012). Daisaku Ikeda's curriculum of Soka education: Creating value through dialogue, global citizenship, and "human education" in the mentor-disciple relationship. *Curriculum Inquiry, 42*(1), 56–79.

Green, M. (1993). *Gandhi: Voice of a new age revolution*. New York: Continuum.

Gundara, J. S. (2003). *Intercultural education: World on the brink?* Professorial Lecture. London: Institute of Education, University of London.

Gundara, J. S., & Sharma, N. (2008, April). Makiguchi and Gandhi: Some comparative issues for sacred, secular and political education. *Comparative and International Education Review, 10,* 70–96.

Gupta, S. R., Schöttli, U., & Axer, J. (Eds.). (1990). *Citizenship values in India: Individualism and social imperatives.* Calcutta: Mandira.

Hardiman, D. (2003). *Gandhi: In his time and ours.* New Delhi: Permanent Black.

Harima, H. (1997). *Yokuwakaru soka kyoiku.* Tokyo: Daisanbunmeisha.

Held, D. (1987). *Models of democracy.* Cambridge: Polity Press.

Henderson, H., & Ikeda, D. (2004). *Planetary citizenship: Your values, beliefs and actions can shape a sustainable world.* Santa Monica, CA: Middleway Press.

Ikeda, D. (1999). The SGI's peace movement. In D. W. Chappell (Ed.), *Buddhist peacework: Creating cultures of peace* (pp. 129–138). Boston: Wisdom Publications and Boston Research Center for the 21st Century.

Ikeda, D. (2001). *Soka education: A Buddhist vision for teachers, students and parents.* Santa Monica, CA: Middleway Press.

Ikeda, D. (2010). *Soka education: For the happiness of the individual* (Rev. ed.). Santa Monica, CA: Middleway Press.

Ito, T. (2005). "'Shonen Nihon' keisai no Yamamoto Shinichiro 'Pesutarocchi' ni tuite (1)" [Shinichiro Yamamoto's publication about Pestalozzi in 'Shonen Nihon' (1)]. *Soka kyoiku kenkyu* [Soka Education Research], *4,* 31–62.

Ito, T. (2007). "'Shonen Nihon' keisai no Yamamoto Shinichiro 'Pesutarocchi' ni tuite (2)" [Shinichiro Yamamoto's publication about Pestalozzi in 'Shonen Nihon' (2)]. *Soka kyoiku kenkyu* [Soka Education Research], *6,* 1–20.

Kress, G., & Leeuwen, T. V. (2001). *Multimodal discourse: The modes and media of contemporary communication.* London: Arnold.

Kumagai, K. (2000). *Tsunesaburo Makiguchi.* Tokyo: Daisanbunmeisha.

Marcuse, H. (1972). *One dimensional man.* London: Abacus.

Markovits, C. (2003). *The un-Gandhian Gandhi.* London: Anthem.

Miller, G. (2002). *Peace, value, and wisdom: The educational philosophy of Daisaku Ikeda.* Amsterdam, the Netherlands: Rodopi.

Nandy, A. (1983). *The intimate enemy: Loss and recovery of self under colonialism.* New Delhi: Oxford University Press.

Obelleiro, G. (2012). A moral cosmopolitan perspective on language education. *Critical Inquiry in Language Studies, 9*(1–2), 33–59.

Parekh, B. (1995). *Gandhi's political philosophy.* New Delhi: Ajanta Publications.

Rawson, W. (Ed.). (1936). *Learning to live together: Report of the Dutch regional conference of the new education fellowship in Untrecht, 14–20 September, 1936.* London: New Education Fellowship.

Schumacher, E. F. (1973). *Small is beautiful: Economics as if people mattered.* London: Blond & Briggs.

Sharma, N. (1999). *Value creators in education: Japanese educator Tsunesaburo Makiguchi & Mahatma Gandhi and their relevance for Indian education* (2nd ed.). New Delhi: Regency Publications.

Sharma, N. (2008). *Makiguchi and Gandhi: Their educational relevance for the 21st century.* Lanham, MD: University Press of America, Rowman & Littlefield.

Swan, M. (1985). *Gandhi: The South African experience.* Johannesburg: Ravan Press.

Watanabe, T. (2000). The movement and the Japanese media. In B. Wilson & D. Machacek (Eds.), *Global citizens: The Soka Gakkai Buddhist movement in the world* (pp. 205–231). Oxford: Oxford University Press.

Check for updates

CHAPTER 3

Global Citizenship Education and Non-Western Perspectives

Abstract The three interrelated domains of learning within United Nations Educational, Scientific and Cultural Organization's (UNESCO's) conceptual dimensions of global citizenship education (GCE) are cognitive, socio-emotional, and behavioral. These correspond to UNESCO's four pillars of learning that are learning to know, to do, to be, and to live together. This chapter contributes to the cognitive dimension of *learning to know* through a study of the Asian thinkers, Makiguchi, Gandhi, and Ikeda. Suggestions are made for curricula to have an intercultural focus and engage with non-Western and less widely known perspectives. This can also enhance the practice of GCE. For instance, alternative ways of thinking about and engaging with others can expand the current focus from individual empowerment to an emphasis on enhancing the capacity within students to live a contributive life.

Keywords Global citizenship education · Cognitive · Non-Western perspectives · Makiguchi · Gandhi · Ikeda

Introduction

This chapter moves forward the discussions in prior chapters to develop a theoretical basis for the practice of value-creating global citizenship education. It situates the arguments made in this book within some of the

N. Sharma, *Value-Creating Global Citizenship Education*,
Palgrave Studies in Global Citizenship Education and Democracy,
https://doi.org/10.1007/978-3-319-78244-7_3

relevant discussions on global citizenship education (GCE). For example, other studies, such as by Dower (2000), have also adopted a more philosophical approach to global citizenship. The over-arching contribution of this study, however, is to respond to the search for "supplementary perspectives" (Andreotti n.d., 2014) to examine diverse pathways and possibilities for the practice of GCE.

To provide some context, Dill's work (2011, 2012, 2013), for instance, expounds the dominant epistemological and ontological assumptions of Western liberal capitalism and its ties to global citizenship education, focusing on the tension that exists within education to respond to the contending interests of the individual and society, self and the other, local and global. It is proposed through my study of the Asian examples an exposition of alternative perspectives that can facilitate what Gaudelli (2009) calls a "dialogic bent" within the curriculum so that students encounter multiple worldviews within classroom processes. As mentioned earlier, this includes different ways of thinking about ourselves, society, nature, and the universe that can add to the intercultural dimension of GCE. This chapter examines the cognitive dimension of *learning to know* and what should be part of the learning experience. It is proposed that the curriculum should represent diverse perspectives. The next section provides a brief background of GCE to position these discussions.

Key Arguments and Debates in Global Citizenship Education

The Global Education First Initiative (GEFI) launched by the United Nations Secretary-General in September 2012 has three aims[1]:

1. Put every child in school.
2. Improve the quality of learning.
3. Foster global citizenship.

Recent comprehensive analyses and conceptual reviews of the term "global citizenship" distinguish it from national citizenship, while also tracing its origins as historically formalized within the broader global education approach, with roots in ancient Greek cosmopolitan visions, modern thought, including Kant and the Enlightenment, the Universal

Declaration of Human Rights (1948) issued after Second World War, and other international agreements that largely aim to protect the basic rights of people across nation-states (see Andreotti and de Souza 2012; Gaudelli 2016; Oxley and Morris 2013; Tarozzi and Torres 2016; Torres 2017).

Also, as has been widely argued, recent developments in information and communication technologies and financial capitalism have given a thrust within most modern nation-states to equip their students with the knowledge, skills, abilities, behaviors, and values required to live and work in this new global order. Under the wing of Global Education various fields that aim to engage with related issues include Development Education, Human Rights Education, Education for Sustainability, Education for Peace and Conflict Prevention, Intercultural and Interfaith Education, and the global dimension of Education for Citizenship (Tarozzi and Torres 2016: 6).

GCE is one of the strategic areas of the United Nations Educational, Scientific and Cultural Organization's (UNESCO's) education sector program for the period 2014–2021. UNESCO's work in this field is guided by the Education 2030 Agenda and Framework for Action, notably Target 4.7 of the Sustainable Development Goals (SDG 4 on education), which calls on countries to ensure that all learners are provided with the knowledge and skills to promote sustainable development, including, among others, through education for sustainable development and sustainable lifestyles, human rights, gender equality, promotion of a culture of peace and non-violence, global citizenship and appreciation of cultural diversity and of culture's contribution to sustainable development.[2]

GCE as a consequence has emerged as a response to these objectives within education systems of the modern world. Research shows that the integration of GCE within schools has varied (Yemini 2017). Further, as Tarozzi and Torres (2016) point out, there are several different approaches to its practice, for example, in Africa, where GCE is seen in the rubric of peace education; in Latin America or the Middle East that have experienced totalitarian regimes or dictatorships, and where civic education prevails; and the case of the Asian Pacific continent where "regional cooperation mechanisms have placed much emphasis on other critical elements of GCE, such as civics and citizenship, democracy and good governance, as well as peace and tolerance" as the standards (Tarozzi and Torres 2016: 6–7).

Also, there is a wide range of existing and emerging definitions of the term global citizenship that are being categorized through recent studies. Oxley and Morris (2013), for instance, review the existing typologies of the global citizenship concept. Drawing upon various ongoing studies Yemini (2017) notes that depending on the definition of global citizenship and the various dispositions and agendas it embodies, the definitions and models of GCE and its focus on its goals in terms of student outcomes changes. Examples given include Andreotti's (2006) differentiation between "soft" and "critical" global citizenship and its effect on global citizenship education.

> While soft GCE could be equated with education that provides students with an understanding of the world and encourages cultural tolerance (as per Marshall, 2011), critical GCE requires deeper engagement. Critical GCE, which Andreotti (2010) later developed into post-critical and post-colonial GCE, requires students and teachers to "unlearn" their previous assumptions regarding the supremacy of Western culture and the distribution of power and replace them with a completely novel understanding of the world. This type of GCE provides students with the skills to reflect upon and engage with global issues involving conflict, power, and opposing views; to understand the nature of assumptions; and to strive for change.
>
> (Yemini 2017: 61)

Parallel to recent studies that outline the broad variety of definitions and outcomes, several critiques of global citizenship as well have emerged along with concerns regarding important issues that include youth participation (Bourn 2016), gender equality, and social justice (Unterhalter 2008). Other scholarly studies address existing gaps between Western—non-Western (Wang and Hoffman 2016); religious—secular (Dill 2013); national—political—cosmopolitan education for global citizenship (Appiah 2008; Parekh 2003); and its relation to theory and praxis (Tarozzi and Torres 2016; Torres 2017; Yemini 2017).

Further, there is wide-ranging scholarship that challenges the Western-dominated agendas and the underlying Western worldview in GCE (Andreotti 2006, 2011; Andreotti and de Souza 2012; Bowden 2003; Calhoun 2002; Dill 2013; Gaudelli 2016; Jooste and Heleta 2017; Merryfield 2009; Tarozzi and Torres 2016; Torres 2017).

The variety of analyses includes post-colonial critiques, studies on the existing pedagogical assumptions within GCE, as well as the need to engage with alternative paradigms and non-Western perspectives.

Jooste and Heleta (2017) for instance argue that "the notion of global citizenship in higher education (HE) is not a viable and desirable proposition for the South, which is largely excluded from the debates about the concept" (ibid.: 39), as well as, the exclusion experienced by the South through various restrictions on mobility and travel. Citing Calhoun (2003) they state, "This has been especially prominent since September 11, 2001. 'The global border control regime encourages a sense of natural cosmopolitanism for some [those from the North] and reminds others of their nationality (and often of religion and ethnicity as well)'" (Calhoun 2003: 543 as cited in Jooste and Heleta 2017: 43). This also raises the important question to "the proponent of global citizenship," as Jooste and Heleta argue, of "whose values and norms will guide global citizens?" (Jooste and Heleta 2017: 44). Instead, the authors call for the development of "socially responsible, ethical and globally competent graduates" rather than global citizens (ibid.: 40), subscribing to Dower's view that global problems, such as conflict, human rights violations, poverty, inequality, and environmental degradation "require individuals to exercise global responsibility" (Dower 2000: 553).

Similarly, Bowden points out that the proponents of cosmopolitanism and global citizenship have in the past only "embraced and advocated...Western liberal democratic values at the expense of non-Western values" (Bowden 2003: 360). As part of its Western worldview there has also been an overt concern with the individual underlying GCE, and according to Dill (2013) this is reflected in the intersections between two defining aspects of consciousness (tolerance, universal benevolence, and human rights) and competencies for GCE (that include technical and dispositional skills for success in the global economy). Several advocates of global citizenship who emphasize both these aspects include UNESCO, The Organization for Economic Co-operation and Development (OECD) through the Programme for International Student Assessment (PISA), academic scholars, organizations, such as the Asia Society, Bill and Melinda Gates Foundation, and other such corporations who share a similar view in America and abroad.

Where and How Do We Fit in Less Widely Known Perspectives?

Given the emerging alternative understandings that inform ongoing research and praxis in GCE it becomes imperative to locate available semantic spaces where substantive non-Western examples can enter the existing discourse.

The three GEFI goals stated in the beginning of this chapter and related UNESCO directives have impacted my long-term work on the relevance of non-Western thinkers. For example, my first book (Sharma 1999) offered suggestions for Education for All (EFA) through a comparative analysis of the ideas of Makiguchi and Gandhi. EFA is an initiative that emerged from UNESCO's movement since 1990 to expand the access to education and is the first GEFI goal. My second book (Sharma 2008), in resonance with the GEFI second goal, advocates a qualitative transformation of schools based on a study of selected educational institutions that are in the lineage of Makiguchi, Ikeda, and Gandhi. This third book is committed to the goal of education for global citizenship as outlined as the third GEFI initiative.

One of the central arguments being made in this work is that the discourse on global consciousness within GCE must, with greater urgency, engage in an ontological and epistemological dialogue with less widely known perspectives. As noted earlier, global citizenship has (for many substantiated reasons) come under scrutiny by several scholars who argue the associated education to be individualistic, hegemonic, and problematic in its attempts to universalize practice across local and national levels. Notwithstanding its current predicament, GCE provides the discursive space that can allow a genuine intercultural understanding of particularities and specificities where universal assumptions are being made within education globally.

Alternative perspectives need to be integrated into the curriculum that can strengthen the existing UNESCO guidelines on topics and objectives for GCE. For example, the cognitive domain, which is described as the "knowledge and thinking skills necessary to better understand the world and its complexities" (UNESCO 2015: 22) can have a multi-dimensional focus. As an example, taking the position by postcolonial scholars, such as Wang and Hoffman (2016), would develop "…a postcolonial global citizenship education grounded on self-reflexive and self-critical epistemologies that deconstruct universalist assumptions and open a space imagination of alternative ways of being and engaging with the world" (ibid.: 6). Similarly, the selected Asian thinkers in this book can also provide an innovate perspective to the current UNESCO topics and guidelines.

As this book argues, the practice of GCE can work best within a curriculum that is non-centric, that represents the knowledge of a varied group of people. This proposal follows from a previous coauthored paper on the topic of sustainable development in higher education, in which it was suggested that whereas sustainable development has often been associated with environmental concerns (Morris 2008), an approach to issues of sustainability from an intercultural perspective can draw from diverse wisdom and understandings that is in line with UNESCO's aims for Education for Sustainable Development (Gundara and Sharma 2010).

Similarly, in this case, the examples of Makiguchi, Gandhi, and Ikeda can contribute to the discourse on global consciousness within GCE through asking important existential questions, such as issues concerned with how we view ourselves, nature, society, and the universe (addressed further in Chapter 4). Common to the Asian philosophies practiced by these thinkers is a framework of thinking that is developed through an intuitive examination of the depth of human life. As Ikeda explains,

> Our worldview is shaped by our consciousness of self. Perceiving that the universe is divided into the self and other – internal and external – arises from our consciousness of self. This consciousness likewise gives rise to other dualities: for example, the duality of mind and body, in which we regard the mind as the true self whereas the body somehow is not; the duality of the material and the spiritual; and the duality of humankind and nature. Modern civilizations evolution under such dualistic thinking is also the root of many of our present conflicts.
>
> (Ikeda 2003b: 106)

As a consequence of this way of thinking, the goal of education within the *soka* paradigm, which is individual happiness, is inextricably linked to other people, that is, an individual cannot become truly happy on one's own. Instead, happiness is found in a life of value creation which is "the capacity to find meaning, to enhance one's own existence and contribute to the well-being of others, under any circumstances" (Ikeda 2008: 443). It is an outcome of sharing in the trials and successes of other persons of one's community (Bethel 1989: 22–25). This inseparable link between the happiness of the self and the welfare of the other permeates the ethos within Soka institutions and has shown to significantly impact the lives of those associated with it (see Nagashima 2016; Seager 2006; Sharma 2008). Using Ikeda's words, this ethos can be described as an "ethic of coexistence…a spirit that seeks to encourage mutual flourishing and mutually supportive relationships among humans and between humans and nature" (Ikeda 2003a: 9).

One of the emerging questions from a study of these thinkers, for example, is how can we develop the capacity within human beings to facilitate the development of a "creative coexistence" (Ikeda 2010: 89). A greater emphasis within Soka Education is arguably therefore on building relationships through the curriculum—between the individual and other people, with nature, and the community (see Goulah 2010: 264–269; Nagashima 2016; Obelleiro 2012: 44; Sharma 2008: 111–116, 145–147). This has important lessons for the current practice of GCE. For instance, the aims outlined by UNESCO (2015: 16) are useful to develop the knowledge, values, skills, and attitudes that can contribute to individual empowerment. Here, the practice of global citizenship can engage with these Asian perspectives to place a greater emphasis on a collective effort to build relationships and the learner's value-creating skills. This proposal and aim is encapsulated in the title and discussions in this book.

These different perspectives can widen the scope of inquiry within the topics and objectives suggested by UNESCO. For example, providing students with the opportunity to discuss issues around existential questions, such as asked within the core curriculum at Soka University of America (Ikeda 2010: 103–104):

- What is an individual human life?
- What is the relationship between the individual and the physical environment in which we live?
- What is the relationship between the individual and the human environment in which we live?
- What are the global issues in peace, culture, and education?

Similar questions might be asked about the nature of the human being, concepts, such as good and evil, and the perspective on duties and rights that emerge from it (see Parekh 1989; Sharma 2008: 63–67). For instance, studying the emergence of Gandhi's political philosophy as an outcome of his ongoing experiments with truth as *dharma* or the law of the universe (see Gandhi 1940).[3] These worthwhile questions also challenge epistemic assumptions when studied from a variety of perspectives and can make important contributions to the discourse on GCE and UNESCO's goal of *learning to know*.

Also, such views lend itself to an implicit trust in the possibility that an individual transformation can directly impact upon the transformation of a society, which is a key aspect in the development of character within the *soka* and *satyagraha* processes (Sharma 2008: 146–147). Character here, as viewed by Gandhi, is a pattern of living based on truth and non-violence (Avinashilingam 1960: 35). As mentioned in an earlier study, for Makiguchi, "a person of character was someone whose existence centered on creating value that enhances to the fullest both personal life and the network of interdependent relationships that constitutes the individual's communal life" (Sharma 2008: 147). Reflecting on Gandhi's legacy for our present time, Ikeda comments,

> His belief in non-violence and justice grew out of his absolute trust in humanity...His method represents the essence of the type of deductive reasoning that, in the characteristic way of Asian philosophy, always begins in a reflective return to the self.
>
> (Ikeda 1996: 130–131)

At the same time, Ikeda also notes that Gandhi was astute in observing that, "Goodness must be joined with knowledge. Mere goodness is not of much use...One must cultivate the fine discriminating quality which goes with spiritual courage and character" (Gandhi 1965: 34 in Ikeda 1996: 135). As the actions taken by these thinkers, Makiguchi, Ikeda, and Gandhi, suggest, they did not disregard the fact that issues of power exist within societies. At the same time, as the study on Gandhi in Chapter 2 of this book demonstrates normative values like non-violence can effectively engage through creative processes even within political realities. Further, as argued in Chapter 5 the contradictions and paradoxes that arise as values engage with politics can be viewed as important lessons within education for citizenship. The argument being made is that historical and modern-day examples of the active engagement of polity within diverse societies and in different time periods can stimulate creative thinking. Bringing these discussions into the classroom is indispensable in order to foster active citizens through the practice of GCE.

One way to bring into focus the contributions of less widely known perspectives or voices from the margins into mainstream education for citizenship is through comparative contextual studies and to develop global themes that can be used in discussions within educational policy and praxis. Chapter 6 undertakes this task. Themes developed integrate the three interrelated domains of learning—the cognitive, socio-emotional, and behavioral. These themes can be used to develop age-specific learning objectives. Further, Chapter 7 makes suggestions to develop new curricula on the selected thinkers and their relevance for GCE.

Conclusion and Moving Forward

To summarize the arguments of this chapter, it engages with the cognitive domain of *learning to know*. The discussions are aimed to contribute to the development of a curriculum that can represent diverse perspectives, such as from the examples of my selected Asian thinkers.

In conclusion, the intent of this chapter can be encapsulated in Makiguchi's vision as outlined by Ikeda as follows, "…in (his book) *Jinsei chirigaku* (The Geography of Human Life) Makiguchi urged international society to enter an age of 'humanitarian competition,' where the aim is to cultivate the spirit of global citizenship and strive for the mutual happiness and benefit of self and other (Makiguchi 1983: 398–401)" (Ikeda 2003a: 21).

All three thinkers address issues that are pertinent to the discourse on GCE, including, on youth participation, the role of women, gender equality, and social justice. These important concerns require a much broader and detailed study through future research. As a start, the next chapter engages with the contribution that Ikeda's ideas can make to the discussion on dialogue and the socio-emotional dimension of *learning to be* within GCE.[4]

Notes

1. http://www.unesco.org/new/en/gefi/about/.
2. Retrieved from http://en.unesco.org/gced/approach.
3. Also as discussed in Chapter 2. For further analysis on Gandhi's political philosophy and his ontological assumptions, see Parekh (1989). Also, see Parekh (2003) on Gandhi and global citizenship education.
4. As examples of Ikeda and the Soka Gakkai International's continued support to the various United Nations directives see, for example, the nuclear abolition initiative: https://peoplesdecade2.wixsite.com/nuclear-abolition.

References

Andreotti, V. (2006). Soft versus critical global citizenship education. *Development Education: Policy and Practice, 3*(Autumn), 83–98.

Andreotti, V. (2010). Global education in the 21st century: Two different perspectives on the post of postmodernism. *International Journal of Development Education and Global Learning, 2*(2), 5–22.

Andreotti, V. (2011). *Actionable postcolonial theory in education*. New York: Palgrave Macmillan.

Andreotti, V. (2014). Towards de(coloniality) and diversality in global citizenship education. In V. Andreotti (Ed.), *The political economy of global citizenship education* (pp. 74–90). Oxon: Routledge.

Andreotti, V. (n.d.). *Engaging the (geo)political economy of knowledge construction: Towards decoloniality and diversality in global citizenship education*. Retrieved from https://www.ucalgary.ca/peacestudies/files/peacestudies/Engaging%20the%20(geo)political%20economy%20of%20knowledge%20construction.pdf.

Andreotti, V., & de Souza, L. (Eds.). (2012). *Postcolonial perspectives on global citizenship education*. New York: Routledge.

Appiah, K. A. (2008). Education for global citizenship. *Yearbook of the National Society for the Study of Education, 107*(1), 83–99.

Avinashilingam, T. S. (1960). *Gandhiji's experiments in education*. New Delhi: Ministry of Education.

Bethel, D. M. (Ed.). (1989). *Education for creative living: Ideas and proposals of Tsunesaburo Makiguchi*. Ames: Iowa State University Press.

Bourn, D. (2016). *Global citizenship and youth participation*. Oxford, UK: Oxfam.

Bowden, B. (2003). The perils of global citizenship. *Citizenship Studies, 7*, 349–362.

Calhoun, C. (2002). The class consciousness of frequent travelers: Toward a critique of actually existing cosmopolitanism. *The South Atlantic Quarterly, 101*, 869–897.

Calhoun, C. (2003). "Belonging" in the cosmopolitan imaginary. *Ethnicities, 3*, 531–568.

Dill, J. S. (2011). *Schooling global citizens: The moral pedagogy of twenty-first century education*. Unpublished doctoral dissertation, Department of Sociology, University of Virginia, Charlottesville, VA.

Dill, J. S. (2012). The moral education of global citizens. *Society, 49*, 541–546.

Dill, J. S. (2013). *The longings and limits of global citizenship education: The modern pedagogy of schooling in a cosmopolitan age*. New York: Routledge.

Dower, N. (2000). The idea of global citizenship: A sympathetic assessment. *Global Society, 14*, 553–567.

Gandhi, M. K. (1940). *An autobiography or the story of my experiments with truth*. Ahmedabad: Navajivan Publishing House.

Gandhi, M. K. (1965). *Gandhi on non-violence: Selected texts from non-violence in peace and war*. New York: New Directions Publishing Corp.

Gaudelli, W. (2009). Heuristics of global citizenship discourses towards curriculum enhancement. *Journal of Curriculum Theorizing, 25*(1), 68–85.

Gaudelli, W. (2016). *Global citizenship education: Everyday transcendence*. New York: Routledge.

Goulah, J. (2010). From (harmonious) community life to (creative) coexistence considering Daisaku Ikeda's educational philosophy in the Parker, Dewey, Makiguchi, and Ikeda "reunion." *Schools: Studies in Education, 7*(2), 253–275. http://www.jstor.org/stable/10.1086/656075.

Gundara, J. S., & Sharma, N. (2010). Interculturalism, sustainable development and higher education institutions. *International Journal of Development Education and Global Learning, 2*(2), 23–34.

Ikeda, D. (1996). Gandhism and the modern world. In *A new humanism: The university addresses of Daisaku Ikeda* (pp. 128–139). New York: Weatherhill.

Ikeda, D. (2003a). *A global ethic of coexistence: Toward a 'life-sized' paradigm for our age*. Tokyo: Soka Gakkai International.

Ikeda, D. (2003b). *Unlocking the mysteries of birth and death...and everything in between: A Buddhist view of life* (2nd ed.). Santa Monica, CA: Middleway Press.

Ikeda, D. (2008). Thoughts on education for global citizenship. In *My dear friends in America: Collected U.S. addresses 1990–1996* (2nd ed., pp. 441–451). Santa Monica, CA: World Tribune Press.

Ikeda, D. (2010). *Soka education: For the happiness of the individual* (Rev. ed.). Santa Monica, CA: Middleway Press.

Jooste, N., & Heleta, S. (2017). Global citizenship versus globally competent graduates: A critical view from the south. *Journal of Studies in International Education, 21*(1), 39–51.

Makiguchi, T. (1983). *Jinsei chirigaku* [The geography of human life]. *Makiguchi Tsunesaburo zenshu* [Complete works of Tsunesaburo Makiguchi] (Vols. 1–2). Tokyo: Daisan Bunmeisha.

Marshall, H. (2011). Instrumentalism, ideals and imaginaries: Theorising the contested space of global citizenship education in schools. *Globalisation, Societies and Education, 9*(3–4), 411–426.

Merryfield, M. (2009). Moving the center of global education: From imperial worldviews that divide the world to double consciousness, contrapuntal pedagogy, hybridity, and cross-cultural competence. In T. F. Kirkwood-Tucker (Ed.), *Visions in global education* (pp. 215–239). New York: Peter Lang.

Morris, L. V. (2008). Higher education and sustainability. *Innovative Higher Education, 32*(179), 180.

Nagashima, J. T. (2016). *The meaning of relationships for student agency in soka education: Exploring the lived experiences and application of Daisaku Ikeda's value–creating philosophy through narrative inquiry*. Unpublished doctoral dissertation, University of Pittsburgh, Pittsburgh, PA.

Obelleiro, G. (2012). A moral cosmopolitan perspective on language education. *Critical Inquiry in Language Studies, 9*(1–2), 33–59. https://doi.org/10.1080/15427587.2012.648064.

Oxley, L., & Morris, P. (2013). Global citizenship: A typology for distinguishing its multiple conceptions. *British Journal of Educational Studies, 61*(3), 301–325.

Parekh, B. (1989). *Gandhi's political philosophy: A critical examination*. London: Macmillan.

Parekh, B. (2003). Cosmopolitanism and global citizenship. *Review of International Studies, 29*, 3–17.

Seager, R. H. (2006). *Encountering the dharma: Daisaku Ikeda, Soka Gakkai, and the globalization of Buddhist humanism*. Berkeley: University of California Press.

Sharma, N. (1999). *Value creators in education: Japanese educator Makiguchi & Mahatma Gandhi and their relevance for the Indian education* (2nd ed.). New Delhi: Regency Publications.

Sharma, N. (2008). *Makiguchi and Gandhi: Their educational relevance for the 21st century*. Lanham, MD: University Press of America, Rowman & Littlefield.

Tarozzi, M., & Torres, C. A. (2016). *Global citizenship education and the crises of multiculturalism: Comparative perspectives*. London: Bloomsbury Academic.

Torres, C. A. (2017). *Theoretical and empirical foundations of critical global citizenship education*. New York: Routledge.

UNESCO, United Nations Educational Scientific and Cultural Organization. (2015). *Global citizenship education: Topics and learning objectives*. Paris: UNESCO.

Unterhalter, E. (2008). Cosmopolitanism, global social justice and gender equality in education. *Compare: A Journal of Comparative and International Education, 38*(5), 539–553.

Wang, C., & Hoffman, D. M. (2016). Are WE the world? A critical reflection on selfhood and global citizenship education. *Education Policy Analysis Archives, 24*(56). http://dx.doi.org/10.14507/epaa.24.2152.

Yemini, M. (2017). *Internationalization and global citizenship: Policy and practice in education*. Cham, Switzerland: Palgrave Macmillan.

CHAPTER 4

Revisiting the Concept of Dialogue in Global Citizenship Education

Abstract As discussed in the previous chapter, the three domains of learning within the global citizenship education conceptual dimensions of United Nations Educational Scientific and Cultural Organization (UNESCO) are the cognitive, socio-emotional, and behavioral, which correspond to the four pillars of learning that are, learning to know, to do, to be, and to live together. This chapter discusses issues related to the socio-emotional dimension of *learning to be* from selected Asian perspectives that develop a sense of interdependence and common humanity, and promote dialogic, reflective, and transformative learning experiences. It examines the contributions that the Japanese thinker, Daisaku Ikeda's ideas can make to revisit the notion of dialogue within global citizenship education and dialogic modes of learning.

Keywords Global citizenship education · UNESCO · Socio-emotional Ikeda · Dialogue · Dialogic

---

This chapter was first published in the *International Journal of Development Education and Global Learning*, volume 3, number 2 (2011), pp. 5–19, Trentham Books Limited, reproduction with permission. Additions and modifications have been made to keep consistency with the arguments, language, and format of this book.

N. Sharma, *Value-Creating Global Citizenship Education*,
Palgrave Studies in Global Citizenship Education and Democracy,
https://doi.org/10.1007/978-3-319-78244-7_4

Introduction

As briefly explored in the previous chapter, these Asian perspectives promote reflective and transformative experiences. This chapter examines this further and explores the implications of this study for the socio-emotional dimension of *learning to be*, which is described by UNESCO (2015: 15) as "a sense of belonging to a common humanity, sharing values and responsibilities, empathy, solidarity and respect for differences and diversity."

In particular, this chapter engages with Ikeda's views and rethinks the role of dialogue in global citizenship education. To begin, a brief comparison is made to selected policy documents on citizenship education in the UK with the aim to engage with issues that are considered to be relevant across modern, democratic nation states.[1]

The discussions here are an outcome of my prior study on the global dimension of citizenship education conducted during my work in higher education in UK. It should be noted that in Japan there is no single consensus or national policy document on citizenship. Various studies are available, for example, on the different politics, interpretations and controversies surrounding citizenship education in Japan since the end of the Second World War (see Ikeno 2011).

Investigating Ontological Paradigms: The Crick Report and Ikeda's View

In 1998, the Crick Report recommendations in UK led to the introduction of citizenship education as a compulsory element of the school curriculum in England and Wales. The report engages with several vital issues related to citizenship. Sections 1.9, 5.4 and 10 of the report draw up guidance on the discussion of controversial issues that may arise in the promotion of pupils' Spiritual, Moral, Social and Cultural (SMSC) development. It is a carefully written document that provides useful tools as guidelines for teachers engaging with controversial issues related to Personal, Social and Health Education (PSHE), SMSC, History, Geography, and English.

However, as I had argued in a previous work (Sharma 2008: 153–154), the report does not look at the complexities of engaging with values that arise from the personal domain that have to do with intercultural education. It advocates that students adopt "a willingness and empathy to perceive and understand the interests, beliefs and viewpoints of others" (Crick 2000a: 57) but does not deal with the issue of challenging and if necessary developing one's own values and beliefs through such interaction (also see Crick 2000b). Also, Humes (2008) identifies both individualistic and collectivist elements in citizenship education which he states can also be seen as a "problem" with the Crick Report:

> On the one hand, it means that the discourse of citizenship connects with the experience of many different people in widely different situations. On the other hand, if it becomes subject to divergent interpretations, it runs the risk of becoming an example of vague, feel-good rhetoric, a term that can mean everything and nothing.
>
> (ibid.: 45)

Crick Report has generated enthusiasm and lead to several discussions on citizenship education in England (see Pearce and Spencer 1999). It has also received several critiques, for example, on its failure to address race, gender, and inequalities that widen the gaps between the various sections of the British society (see Osler 2000). One of the outcomes of these various debates has led to the development of the Ajegbo Report (DfES 2007) which has made certain contributions to citizenship education, but has also come under some criticism. As Osler (2008) notes,

> Following the 2005 London bombings, there is widespread public debate about diversity, integration, and multiculturalism in Britain, including the role of education in promoting national identity and citizenship. In response to official concerns about terrorism, a review panel was invited to consider how ethnic, religious and cultural diversity might be addressed in the school curriculum for England, specifically through the teaching of modern British social and cultural history and citizenship. The resultant Ajegbo report proposes a new strand on "identity and diversity: living together in the UK" be added to the citizenship education framework. While the report gives impetus to teaching about diversity, it does not strengthen the curriculum framework proposed in the Crick Report. It fails to adopt a critical perspective on race or multiculturalism or adequately engage with young people's lived experiences of citizenship within a globalised world.
>
> (ibid.: i)

It can also be argued, that although both the Crick and Ajegbo Reports aim to address education in a multicultural society, neither of them offers clarity on the relation between the "self" and the "other." The former vaguely refers to the moorings of the individual's family and community, but does not, for instance, engage with related issues; while the latter contributes to a discussion of values in a diverse society, but fails to recognize the politics of living together with the other (as discussed in Chapter 2 and further developed in Chapter 5). For example, one can argue that a significant problem within most nation states is an increase in the number of insular communities that have mushroomed that in some extreme cases even nurture terrorism. Bauman (1989) refers to this state, in general terms, as our global "risk society" (ibid.: 230). These communities attract the youth by empowering them with a sense of mission for which they are even prepared to sacrifice their own life. These and other related issues of social concern are the macro politics of education which affects citizenship education. Alongside there are the micro politics of education that need to be addressed, such as the sense of alienation and disempowerment that pose challenges for the youth. The role of the institution is of particular relevance, which I will engage with in further detail in the ensuing section.

The emphasis on these issues is especially important now, as Bourn suggests, that in spite of the increased political response to "extremism" in the country, and while promoting "British Values," there has been less emphasis on citizenship education policies and cuts are being made for programs that relate to youth participation with only increased support in the area of volunteering (Bourn 2016: 23). Within formal education the status of Citizenship as a curriculum subject has declined, and "the global element has been dropped with the focus much more on civics (political systems) at the national level" (ibid.).

How do we integrate a global worldview that is integral to social and political engagement? In a previous work (Sharma 2002), I had juxtaposed the "reductionist" Newtonian-Cartesian paradigm, with the "holistic" views of selected thinkers from the East and West so as to find a more cohesive understanding of values. As stated in this writing,

> The central flaw of scientific/industrial development is that it envisages the human being as a cog in a materialistic machine and as a tool to meet its ends. In the words of Fritjof Capra: "Matter was thought to be the basis of all existence, and the material world was seen as a multitude of separate objects assembled into a huge machine. Like human-made machines, the

> cosmic machine was thought to consist of elementary parts. Consequently it was believed that complex phenomena could always be understood by reducing them to their basic building blocks and by looking for the mechanisms through which these interacted. This attitude, known as reductionism, has become so deeply ingrained in our culture that it has often been identified with the scientific method" (Capra 1983: 32). The 'reductionist' worldview, whose imprint predominates in contemporary education, has acted to alienate human life from its natural and social environment.
>
> (Sharma 2002: 99)

In this study I contrasted the "reductionist worldview" to the philosophies of Makiguchi, Gandhi, and John Dewey (1859–1952). In this chapter, I will concentrate on highlighting some of the ideas of Makiguchi's successor Ikeda.

In many of his peace proposals submitted to the United Nations, Ikeda has written about the Sustainable Development Goals (SDGs). Ikeda's two writings are selected as being pertinent to the discourse on global citizenship and sustainable development being made in this book. The first is his speech delivered in 1996 at Columbia University (Ikeda 2008) that engages with the concept of "global citizens" at length (discussed in this chapter). The second is his 2014 proposal to the United Nations on the occasion of the 2002 World Summit on Sustainable Development (WSSD) (Ikeda 2014) (that informs Chapters 6 and 8 of this book).

In contrast to the above mentioned reductionist paradigm, Ikeda proposes a cosmic view that I would like to elaborate upon in this chapter as an example of an innovative perspective that can facilitate our re-examination of the role of dialogue in global citizenship education. For instance, while acknowledging the contribution made by Descartes to modern European philosophy, Ikeda notes that, "Cartesianism, while it may provide for the untrammelled autonomy of the individual, it is almost entirely devoid of reference to an 'other'..." (1991a: 2). Central to understanding Ikeda's cosmic view is the concept of "dependent origination." In his words,

> One of the most important Buddhist concepts, dependent origination holds that all beings and phenomena exist or occur in relation to other beings or phenomena. Everything is linked to an intricate web of causation and connection – and nothing – whether in the realm of human affairs or of natural phenomena – can exist or occur solely of its own accord. In this view, a greater emphasis is placed on the interdependent relationships between individuals than on the individual in isolation.
>
> (Ikeda 1991b: 4)

Although Western observers as Henri Bergson and Alfred Whitehead have noted the interrelatedness, Ikeda states that, "The deeper essence of Buddhism, however, goes beyond this to offer a view of interrelatedness that is uniquely dynamic, holistic, and inner-generated" (ibid.). As illustrated through the Buddhist concept of *esho funi* which describes the non-dualistic relationship between the "self" and its "environment,"

> Buddhism regards life and its environment as two integral aspects of the same entity. The subjective world of the self and the objective world of its environment are not seen in opposition, or as a duality. Their relationship is one of inseparability and indivisibility. Nor is this unity of self and its environment a static one in which these two realms merge as they come objectified. The environment, which embraces all universal phenomena, cannot exist except in a dynamic relation with the internally-generated activity of life itself. For us, in practical terms, the most important question is how to activate the inner sources of energy and wisdom existing within our lives.
> (ibid.: 5)

A key feature here of the individual self is that it is constantly in engagement with, affecting, and being transformed by its environment. The existential questions that emerge from adopting this position of how we perceive our place in this world as human beings merits further engagement in generating a new discourse on identity, self-worth, and related issues. This discourse also relates to student's health and well-being, including, a deeper understanding of student anxiety that can arguably benefit from a change in our approach to existential realities.

Moving on to Ikeda's suggestions for dialogue, he gives the example of Shakyamuni (Gautam) Buddha's ability as a "peerless master of dialogue" because of his ability to observe within the hearts of people "the arrow of a discriminatory consciousness, an unreasoning emphasis on difference…such as ethnicity and nationality" (Ikeda 1993: 2). He further explains that,

> The conquest of our own prejudicial thinking, our own attachment to difference, is the guiding principle for open dialogue, the essential condition for the establishment of peace and universal respect for human rights.
> (ibid.: 3)

Ikeda also acknowledges that dialogue sometimes has to be quite strict to "break the grip of arrogance has on another" (ibid.). In a lecture delivered at Harvard University in 1991 he advocates that it is only through an "inner and outer dialogue between one's 'self' and a profoundly internalized 'other'...can we begin to grasp and fully affirm the reality of being alive" (Ikeda 2010: 57). Further, in reference to Makiguchi's 1903 work, *The Geography of Human Life* (Makiguchi 2002), he emphasizes the relation between humans and the natural environment, that necessitates, among other things, to examine the influence of the natural environment on the development of the personality (ibid.: 89).

Here we need to acknowledge that there are other novel philosophies as well that expound the relation between the "self" and the "other" that can create substantive forms of dialogue, such as, Martin Buber's significant contribution in this endeavor in terms of the "I-Thou" relationship and its function in promoting dialogue between equals as distinguished from the "I-It" relation (see Morgan 2007). Paulo Freire and other critical pedagogues who have emphasized the need for dialogue in education also deserve to be recognized. For the purpose of developing the arguments made in this book, this chapter concentrates on examining a less widely known Eastern philosophy and its proposed contribution to global citizenship education.

In addition to the above discussed cosmic view that is central to Ikeda's ontology, a key focus in his work is given to "humanism." Ikeda makes a distinction between his own understanding of this term as compared to individualist humanism that had been developed in the West over the course of the Renaissance and the Protestant Reformation. He states,

> While these different forms of humanism succeeded in liberating humanity from its medieval thraldom to the Absolute, humanity thus liberated found itself trapped by its own egotism, by what Buddhism calls the 'lesser self.' Humanity has thus come to be ordered about by the dictates of desire and its gratification. The ills that result take the form of the complex of problems facing humanity already referred to: the unravelling of social and community ties, environmental degradation, the growing gap between rich and poor. The depth of the crisis gripping our post-ideological world is powerfully symbolized by the emergence of a wide range of fundamentalism.
>
> (Ikeda 1997: 4)

Here I will not go into the details and debates on humanistic ideologies but aim to suggest instead that Ikeda proposes (what he calls) a "new humanism"[2] to move beyond the present impasse. He asserts that,

> Ideology, which in one form or other has been at the heart of modern humanism, tends to emphasize dualism and conflict, producing discrimination and rejection of others. Cosmologies, in contrast, seek to include and embrace others; tolerance is inherent in cosmology.
>
> (ibid.)

To overcome mistrust Ikeda proposes a "holistic, or even cosmological humanism, one that regards the life of the individual human as extending out to and embracing the entire cosmos, and therefore meriting the most profound reverence" (Ikeda 1997: 5). Ikeda seeks in "education" the "means by which to actualize a universal respect for the sanctity of life" (ibid., also see Ikeda 2001). He maintains that,

> What our world most requires now is the kind of education that fosters love for humankind, that develops character – that provides an intellectual basis for the realization of peace and empowers learners to contribute to and improve society.
>
> (Ikeda 1997: 5)

The Context for Dialogue and Development Within Educational Institutions

In order to develop the context for dialogue within global citizenship education, there needs to be not only a facilitation of verbal communication but also the processes of learning must be dialogic (see Bourn 2014; Gaudelli 2009; Kumar 2008). For instance, the knowledge within the curriculum should provide students the opportunity to engage with different perspectives (as discussed in Chapter 3).

Of equal importance is the role of educational institutions to facilitate students' experiences of sustained engagement in the activities of their local communities, as for example being done within the Soka Schools.

These schools are heavily impacted by normative values such as peace and human rights, and aim to "foster global citizens."[3] Ikeda's speech delivered in Columbia University engages with the concept of "global citizens" at length and identifies it with the Buddhist term *Bodhisattva* (Ikeda 2008: 445).[4] Briefly, Bodhisattva is the life state that exists as an innate potential within human lives, and causes people to take action to alleviate the sufferings of others. As Takazawa explains, "This life condition is also the closest to the happiness that characterizes Buddhist enlightenment" (Takazawa 2016: 10). Ikeda lists the essential elements of global citizenship as:

- the wisdom to perceive the interconnectedness of all life and living;
- the courage not to fear or deny difference but to respect and strive to understand people of different cultures and to grow from such encounters with them;
- the compassion to maintain an imaginative empathy that reaches beyond one's immediate surroundings and extends to those suffering in distant places.

As I had previously explored in another article, the term *Bodhisattva* is key to Ikeda's Soka Education system and suggests the description of a global citizen to be "a human being endowed with courage, compassion and wisdom who, as an active citizen, concentrates on the positive transformation of one's own life, and therefore transforms one's nation and humanity" (Sharma 2007). One of the powerful contributions of these institutional values is the sense of mission and trust that students experience within the Soka Schools (Sharma 2008). Further, Ikeda's philosophy is shared within the lay Buddhist movement, the Soka Gakkai, which has also been actively engaged in Japanese politics through providing political endorsement to the Komeito political party.

The key contributions made by Ikeda's philosophy in real-world education, society, and politics in Japan are down to two points. First, the individual is given top priority in Ikeda's philosophy. As he states,

> It is my view, however, that, the root of all of these problems is our collective failure to make the human being – human happiness – the consistent focus and goal in all fields of endeavor. The human being is the point to which we must return and from which we must depart anew. What is required is a human transformation – a human revolution.
>
> (Ikeda 2008: 443)

Stemming from Ikeda's ontological perspective, while the "other" plays an important role in the construction of the "self," the premise for creating change begins with the individual. The responsibility of the individual toward the other is a function of cosmological humanism, that is, a sense of reverence to the web of interdependent relations that exists between individual human beings (see Ikeda 2014). In practical terms, and this brings us to the second point of the success of Soka institutions, is that there is a great deal of thrust on accountability within the leadership of these institutions which is of particular significance. Fisker-Nielson's (2012) anthropological study of Japanese politics indicates Komeito's thrust on social and welfare policies, as my long-term study of Soka Schools shows an emphasis on a student-centered learning (Sharma 2008).

The concept of interdependence itself is not entirely new, and has been a topic of discussion key to development education. For example, Andreotti and Warwick (2007) illustrate that the United Kingdom government Department for International Development (DFID),[5] states that going beyond an attitude of compassion and charity toward the "South" is key to a better informed understanding of this concept and the connections between global processes and people's everyday lives. However, Andreotti and Warwick also argue that the term "interdependence" here can be interpreted in many different ways. These interpretations define the goals and approaches in educational processes, therefore, unpacking assumptions and examining implications are extremely important for informed citizenship education decisions (ibid.: 4).

Dobson (2005) also challenges the concepts of a "global citizen," "interdependence," and "world-wide interconnectedness" that often accompanies unexamined notions of a common humanity in global citizenship education. He addresses the grounds for global citizenship and the notions of a "global citizen" and "interdependence," and proposes that the answer should be framed around political obligation for doing justice; and the source of this obligation should be a recognition of complicity or "causal responsibility" in transnational harm based on a moral obligation to a common humanity, rather than on a political responsibility for the causes of poverty. Dobson also makes a distinction between being human and being a citizen: being human raises issues of morality; being a citizen raises political issues.

Further, a greater attention needs to be given to education that enables students to take action based on understanding the "other," and to develop one's own values and perspectives through the process of dialogue.

Various studies suggest that students across different countries are interested in contributing to positive world change, which institutions need to recognize and develop. For example, research in UK higher education has shown that a vast number of youth are interested in creating change for social justice (Ahier et al. 2003). Previous research on global and sustainability issues for engineering graduates from a sample taken across both old and new universities in UK showed that youth are genuinely concerned about the impact of climate change and global poverty (Bourn and Sharma 2008). In addition, the results of an internal study done by a team at the University of Nottingham show that business graduates are interested to learn more about issues concerning Corporate Social Responsibility (Murphy and Sharma 2009).

It therefore becomes a moral responsibility for educational institutions to nurture the minds of students to contribute to the betterment of their societies, for instance in tandem with the UNESCO adage that war resides in the minds of people, and it is there that the sentinels of peace must be constructed. The role of institutions and the care they provide for students is of particular importance as Noddings points out,

> We really cannot care for people at a great distance without some means of direct contact. *Caring for*, as I have described it (Noddings 1984, 2002), requires us to respond to the expressed needs and to monitor the effects of our actions and react anew to the responses of those we care for. This does not mean that we cannot *care about* many people for whom we cannot care directly. *Caring about* requires us to work toward the establishment of conditions under which caring for can flourish.
>
> (Noddings 2005: 7)

As Noddings mentions, it is also caring for the future. "…learning how to conduct ourselves as global citizen-carers is a major educational task" (ibid.).

Similarly, as Hicks (2002: 18) suggests, learning in schools and in the establishment of Higher Education is still considered a cognitive affair with some attention given to attitude and values. Instead he suggests that global issues and other fields related to the exploration of the human condition have cognitive, affective, and existential dimensions. This raises the crucial question about the role of education in promoting empowerment and action for change as also suggested by Huckle, Jones, Kaza, Macy, and other such thinkers (ibid.).

As White suggests, whereas some schools give the undesirable message to students such as "this institution doesn't trust you, respect you, and so on…it is a sociological truism that the culture of institutions, to a large degree, shapes, for good or ill, the aspirations, habits, and dispositions of those who work in them" (White 1996: 5).

Reflections, Conclusion, and Moving Forward

These are some issues that arise in rethinking education and institutional change from a range of perspectives that are not currently represented within most policies and programs for citizenship. The discourse and practice of global citizenship education should also generate philosophical discussions that enable students to understand the expansiveness of their own lives from a cosmological point of view. For instance, the sense of interdependence and common humanity inherent in the Asian perspectives studied in this chapter can further the discussions on *learning to be* and promote dialogic, reflective, and transformative learning experiences. In meeting global competencies there can be too much focus in education to the achievement and attainment of grades within schools. On the other hand, thinkers like Nussbaum explain some of the merits of studying philosophy to citizenship by allowing learners to open up their minds.

> When we ask about the relationship of a liberal education to citizenship, we are asking a question with a long history in the Western philosophical tradition. We are drawing on Socrates' concept of 'the examined life,' on Aristotle's notions of reflective citizenship, and above all on Greek and Roman Stoic notions of an education that is 'liberal' in that it liberates the mind from the bondage of habit and custom, producing people who can function with sensitivity and alertness as citizens of the world.
>
> (Nussbaum 1997: 8)

Also, by studying the lives of thinkers who have been engaged in their respective societies, students can reflect on their strategies, behaviors, and beliefs as citizens. Chapter 5 engages with this and the goal of *learning to do*. It makes suggestions for educators to consider in enabling students to become active citizens through their classroom experience.

Notes

1. The terms "citizenship education" and "global citizenship" are used as is appropriate within the discussions that are engaged with Ikeda's proposals on education for global citizenship, and UK policy documents on citizenship education.
2. For example, in the title and content of the book that is a collection of some of his university addresses (Ikeda 1996).
3. See http://www.soka.ed.jp/english/.
4. In Mahayana Buddhism, practiced by the Soka Gakkai, the term *Bodhisattva* depicts a state of life that lies within every human being. It emphasizes an ideal of human behavior. It is a state of wisdom,

compassion, and courage by which one can overcome the restraints of egoism and work for the welfare of self and others (see www.sgi.org and Takazawa 2016: 10–14).

5. DFID engages with Britain's aid to poor countries.

References

Ahier, J., Beck, J., & Moore, R. (2003). *Graduate citizens: Issues of citizenship and higher education*. London: Routledge Falmer.

Andreotti, V., & Warwick, P. (2007). Engaging students with controversial issues through a dialogue based approach. *Citized*. Retrieved from http://www.citized.info/?r_menu=res&strand=3.

Bauman, Z. (1989). *Modernity and the holocaust*. Cambridge: Polity.

Bourn, D. (2014). *The theory and practice of global learning* (Development Education Research Centre Research Paper No. 11). London: DERC, Institute of Education & Global Learning Programme.

Bourn, D. (2016). *Global citizenship and youth participation in Europe*. Oxford: Oxfam UK.

Bourn, D., & Sharma, N. (2008, September). The role of engineers being positive in world change: Issues and concerns of engineering graduates in UK. *Municipal Engineer, ICE Proceedings of the Institution of Civil Engineers, 3*, 199–206.

Capra, F. (1983). *The turning point*. London: Flamingo.

Crick, B. (2000a). *Citizenship for 16–19 year olds in education and training: Report of the advisory group to the secretary of state for education and employment*. Coventry: Further Education Funding Council.

Crick, B. (2000b). *Essays on citizenship*. London: Continuum.

DfES. (2007). *Curriculum review: Diversity and citizenship* (Ajegbo report). Nottingham: DfES.

Dobson, A. (2005). Globalisation, cosmopolitanism and the environment. *International Relations, 19*, 259–273.

Fisker-Nielsen, A. M. (2012). *Religion and politics in contemporary Japan: Soka Gakkai youth and Komeito*. Japan Anthropology Workshop Series. London: Routledge.

Gaudelli, W. (2009). Heuristics of global citizenship discourses towards curriculum enhancement. *Journal of Curriculum Theorizing, 25*(1), 68–85.

Hicks, D. (2002). *Lessons for the future: The missing dimension in education*. London: Routledge.

Humes, W. (2008). The discourse of global citizenship. In M. A. Paters, A. Britton, & H. Blee (Eds.), *Global citizenship education: Philosophy, theory and pedagogy* (pp. 41–52). Rotterdam: Sense Publishers.

Ikeda, D. (1991a). *Arousing a new global awareness*. Lecture delivered at the University of East Asia, Macau on January 30, 1991. Retrieved from http://www.daisakuikeda.org/sub/resources/works/lect/lect-02.html.

Ikeda, D. (1991b). *The age of 'soft power' and inner-motivated philosophy*. Lecture delivered at Harvard University, Cambridge, MA, USA on September 26. Retrieved from http://www.daisakuikeda.org/sub/resources/works/lect/lect-02.html.

Ikeda, D. (1993). *Mahayana Buddhism and twenty-first century civilization*. Lecture delivered at Harvard University on September 24. Retrieved from http://www.daisakuikeda.org/sub/resources/works/lect/lect-04.html.

Ikeda, D. (1996). *A new humanism: The university addresses of Daisaku Ikeda*. New York: Weatherhill.

Ikeda, D. (1997). *A new humanism for the coming century*. Lecture delivered at Rajiv Gandhi Institute for Contemporary Studies, New Delhi on October 21. Retrieved from http://www.daisakuikeda.org/sub/resources/works/lect/lect-09.html.

Ikeda, D. (2001). *Soka education: A Buddhist vision for teachers, students and parents*. Santa Monica, CA: Middleway Press.

Ikeda, D. (2008). Thoughts on education for global citizenship. In *My dear friends in America: Collected U.S. addresses 1990–1996* (2nd ed., pp. 441–451). Santa Monica, CA: World Tribune Press.

Ikeda, D. (2010). *Soka education: For the happiness of the individual* (Rev. ed.). Santa Monica, CA: Middleway Press.

Ikeda, D. (2014, January 26). 2014 peace proposal. Value creation for global change: Building resilient and sustainable societies. *Soka Gakkai International Newsletter, SGINL 8935*. Retrieved from http://www.sgi.org/content/files/about-us/president-ikedas-proposals/peaceproposal2014.pdf.

Ikeno, N. (Ed.). (2011). *Citizenship education in Japan*. London: Continuum.

Kumar, A. (2008). Development education and dialogic learning in the 21st century. *International Journal of Development Education and Global Learning, 1*(1), 37–48.

Makiguchi, T. (2002). *A geography of human life* (English ed.). San Francisco, CA: Caddo Gap Press.

Morgan, J. W. (2007). Martin Buber: Philosopher of dialogue and of the resolution of conflict. *British Academy Review, 10*, 11–14.

Murphy, R., & Sharma, N. (2009, Spring). Paradise island as a teaching innovation. *The hub: Learning and teaching at Nottingham*, pp. 25–26. Retrieved from http://www.nottingham.ac.uk/academicservices/documents/thehub-spring09.pdf.

Noddings, N. (1984). *Caring, a feminine approach to ethics & moral education*. Berkeley, CA: University of California Press.

Noddings, N. (2002). *Starting at home: Caring and social policy*. Berkeley, CA: University of California Press.

Noddings, N. (Ed.). (2005). *Educating citizens for global awareness*. New York: Teachers College Press.

Nussbaum, M. C. (1997). *Cultivating humanity: A classical defense of reform in liberal education*. Cambridge, MA: Harvard University Press.

Osler, A. (2000). The crick report: Difference, equality and racial justice. *The Curriculum Journal, 11*(1), 25–37.

Osler, A. (2008). Citizenship education and the Ajegbo report: Re-imagining a cosmopolitan nation. *London Review of Education, 6*(1), 11–25.

Pearce, N., & Spencer, S. (1999). Education for citizenship: The crick report. *The Political Quarterly, 70*, 219–224.

Sharma, N. (2002). Value creation, sarvodaya & participatory democracy: Three legacies for a better way of life. *Social Change, Journal of the Council for Social Development, 32*, 99–116.

Sharma, N. (2007, June). Soka education: Fostering global citizens. *Art of Living, 72*, 8–10.

Sharma, N. (2008). *Makiguchi and Gandhi: Their educational relevance for the 21st century*. Lanham, MD: University Press of America, Rowman & Littlefield.

Sharma, N. (2011). Revisiting the concept of dialogue in global citizenship education. *The International Journal of Development Education and Global Learning, 3*(2), 5–19.

Takazawa, M. (2016). *Exploration of soka education principles on global citizenship: A qualitative study of U.S. K-3 soka educators*. Unpublished doctoral dissertation. The University of San Francisco, San Francisco. Retrieved from http://repository.usfca.edu/diss/324.

UNESCO, United Nations Educational Scientific and Cultural Organization. (2015). *Global citizenship education: Topics and learning objectives*. Paris: UNESCO.

White, P. (1996). *Civic virtues and public schooling: Educating citizens for a democratic society*. New York: Teachers College Press.

CHAPTER 5

Can Active Citizenship Be Learned? Examining Content and Activities in a Teacher's Education Module Engaging with Gandhi and Makiguchi

Abstract This chapter continues this book's engagement with the three domains of learning within the global citizenship education conceptual dimensions of the United Nations Educational, Scientific, and Cultural Organization (UNESCO), which are the cognitive, socio-emotional, and behavioral. In particular, it explores the behavioral dimension of *learning to do* that involves a critical analysis of what it means to be an active citizen. For instance, a study of the Asian thinkers, Tsunesaburo Makiguchi, Daisaku Ikeda, and Mahatma Gandhi shows that there are political implications of taking action based on values, such as peace and non-violence. This chapter starts to develop questions for classroom teaching from the study of these three thinkers and provides segue into the praxis chapters in the next part of this book.

Keywords Global citizenship education · Behavioral · Active citizen Makiguchi · Ikeda · Gandhi

This chapter was first published in *Policy Futures in Education* (Sage Journals), volume 13, number 3 (2015), pp. 328–341, https://doi.org/10.1177/1478210315571215, reproduction with permission. Modifications have been made to keep consistency with the arguments, language, and format of this book.

N. Sharma, *Value-Creating Global Citizenship Education*,
Palgrave Studies in Global Citizenship Education and Democracy,
https://doi.org/10.1007/978-3-319-78244-7_5

Introduction

The aim of UNESCO's core conceptual dimension of *learning to do* is to enable students "to act effectively and responsibly at local, national and global levels for a more peaceful and sustainable world" (UNESCO 2015: 15). In engaging with this behavioral dimension, this chapter will offer a critical analysis of what it means to be an active citizen. It revisits in further depth some issues raised earlier in this book in relation to a study of these thinkers and suggests that there are political implications of taking action based on values, such as peace and non-violence.

The first part of this chapter takes excerpts from an article in which I have argued whether or not active citizenship can be meaningfully fostered within the classrooms of most modern democratic nation states (Sharma 2012). In that publication, I highlighted the contributions that liberal arts colleges can make to develop critical understandings and other necessary attributes and skills for active citizenship in the twenty-first century. This chapter develops such arguments while reflecting on the teaching contents and methods that can be used within citizenship education, with reference to a module that I designed for a postgraduate certificate course at the University of Nottingham in the UK with invaluable inputs from Professor Paul Thompson at the School of Education. The module combines reading material and activities for reflective learning on citizenship education, taking examples of Makiguchi and Gandhi, and with reference to the ideas and work of Ikeda.

Before moving on, some examples are given here about teaching issues around citizenship in India with reference to the use of ideas from Gandhi and his values. It is no exaggeration to suggest that since the independence of India in 1947, educational policies and aims have moved away significantly from Gandhi's approach to education. At the same time, Western education and research has continued to influence Indian education. In the twenty-first century, as citizenship education has become a prominent issue in the educational debates across the world, in India as well attempts have been made to include citizenship education within the diverse school curriculums. As I had mentioned in an earlier writing (Sharma 2008):

> A review of the *Consultation paper on effectuation of fundamental duties of citizens* by *The National Commission to Review the Working of the Constitution* (Advisory Panel 2001) published in 2003 shows that the

> discussion on citizenship values is part of the all too often lack of scholarly use of concepts from ancient Hindu, Jain and Buddhist texts that are given no translation or practical use within the existing political structure or the educational systems. Interestingly the above document on citizenship education highlights the need for Gandhi's ideas and values. It is the only relevant discussion in education on 'redeeming' Gandhi.
>
> However, the socio-political structure in which the attempt is made to bring back Gandhi is different from that suggested by him. The key Gandhian concept invoked in this document is 'duty bound rights,' that is, rights must evolve from carrying out one's duty. The Indian constitution however views duties and rights separately – article 51A deals with the fundamental duties and articles 12 to 35 of part III of the preamble to the constitution of India contain the fundamental rights of an Indian citizen. The consequence of this paradoxical situation, it can be hypothesized, will end up with one of the following options being exercised in the ongoing discussions on citizenship: the futile attempt to invoke Gandhi will be abandoned, or an attempt will be made to address his ideas and values through citizenship education (...in which these values are largely estranged), or as has been till now, discussions and debates on citizenship education will take place outside the curriculum, while instead schools continue to run classes on 'civic education' in which students are provided a general and theoretical understanding of the constitution and political structure of India.
>
> (ibid.: 132)

There is need to engage with Gandhi, as with other such dissident thinkers in education, that can be useful to ameliorate the role of knowledge and values in politics, and allow us to re-think what can be achieved through global citizenship education.

Since 2008, there have been significant developments in terms of a new policy framework that engages with citizenship education in teacher's education, including the national curriculum framework for teacher education 2009 with the final text released in March 2010. As Cappelle et al. (2011: 11) explain, with regard to citizenship education the new framework emphasizes the need to re-conceptualize citizenship training in terms of human rights and approaches of critical pedagogy. It also puts an emphasis on teaching about the environment and its protection, living in harmony with oneself and with the natural and social environment, promotes peace and a democratic way of life, and creates respect for the constitutional values of equality, justice, liberty, fraternity, tolerance, secularism, and empathy. However, this study also shows that there are many youths who are still left out of the discussions as there is often little recognition given by teachers and policy makers to the status of students, especially those who come from socially and economically deprived backgrounds and minority communities.

Dissidents and Their Movements[1]

I begin this section with the premise that *education can* enable young people to understand their rights, obligations, and responsibilities as active citizens within most complex democratic societies. However, we are aware that learning in the classrooms alone does not necessarily lead to developing students as active participants in their local communities or enable them to think as global citizens.

In fact, good examples of citizenship can sometimes be found through civil movements of engaged citizens who have simply arisen to the occasion to fight for justice and human rights because of their particular grievance. For example, we could cite the case of the civil rights movement in the United States, or the *chipko* movement in India, during which ordinary people embraced trees to shield them from being cut down.

The questions this chapter raises are these: who is a citizen?; what does it mean to be an active citizen?; and under what social, political, or educational scenario does a person become a citizen?

So, who is a citizen? A general agreement that we can reach given the various synonyms for this term within different cultural contexts is that in modern democratic nation states a citizen is a resident with responsibilities, as well as certain legal and political rights, including the right to vote. Within the widening debates on teaching and learning in citizenship education, some have looked at engaging with examples of people who have contributed to their community, such as Nelson Mandela and Eleanor Roosevelt. In similar terms should we be concerned with other citizens—like Makiguchi and Gandhi? What do they have to offer?

Gandhi, King, Mandela, Makiguchi who are today seen as global citizens were (actually) trouble makers for their own governments. This paradox makes us re-think key questions in relation to the practice of citizenship education and the discourse on global citizenship education. For example, under what socio-political context is a person driven to take action as a citizen? The people cited here were working in the context of authoritarianism.

Even within a democratic society, there are examples of people who have creatively challenged political and educational processes to promote change. As illustrated by Ikeda and the Soka Gakkai who have confronted various forms of opposition and have emerged as the largest lay Buddhist group in Japan. Also, as compared to Makiguchi's educational influence, Ikeda's value-creating education has had a broader impact within educational institutions that aim to foster responsible citizens of the world. Further, his activities have included conducting extensive dialogues on diverse topics with world leaders from across a variety of fields, while building institutions that promote peace, culture, and education. His many honorary doctorates and citizenship from hundreds of universities and nations are also recognition of the efforts being made by the members of the Buddhist organization. One of the significant results of such activities has included the Soka Gakkai International members' efforts worldwide to engage with global issues within their respective regions, such as the development of youth-led campaigns for the abolition of nuclear weapons within local communities across nation states.[2]

Similarly, Gandhi was able to galvanize millions of youth during the liberation struggle (Sharma 2008: 131–132). Of course, as mentioned earlier through the example of Gandhi's role in Indian politics and the Soka Gakkai members' endorsement of the Komeito party in Japan, a study of such movements often shows that there are political challenges that occur when one tries to create a change within the given power structures. In similar terms, Richard Rorty (1998) in his work *Achieving our country: Leftist thought in twentieth-century America* favors small campaigns over larger movements particularly because he claims "... movements are dangerous to their partisans, ineffective in achieving concrete forms, and performatively self-contradictory over the long term" (Green 2004: 64).

However, although I agree that there are challenges that movements will have to contend with in real-world politics, I argue that two important aspects need consideration. The first is this: although such movements may seem idealistic or naïve in the face of the given political realities, it can also be argued that active participation can lead to an education of the members. The benefit of such ideals for the members (of working for peace or liberty), is not as much in the realization of the goal (because society moves according to the dictates of other factors), but that in the process of working on their ideals the body politic obtains political awareness, that is, they are "educated" in the broader sense of the term.

My second claim is that an examination of the personal histories and political movements of thinkers like Makiguchi and Gandhi is useful to ameliorate the role of knowledge and values in citizenship education. I will elaborate this point through the rest of this chapter.

Let us take the example of Gandhi to elucidate some of these issues. As mentioned in Chapter 2, in a previous study I had argued that Gandhi as an active citizen displayed two key aspects (Sharma 2008). The first was Gandhi the person for whom truth and non-violence was his creed. These normative values were key to the success of his movement known as *satyagraha*.[3] There has been an attempt to engage with this aspect of Gandhi in Indian education. However, this has been problematic. For instance, in 2001, within the controversial re-writing of history textbooks, Gandhi's non-violence was portrayed as a "weakness" by fundamentalists. This was eventually challenged and overturned by leading historians (Delhi Historians' Group 2001: 24), although admittedly there is still no significant engagement with the work of Gandhi in any of the national curriculums in India.

Then there was the second Gandhi, the great soul or *Mahatma*, the moral leader and a nationalist, who had to work through the problematic intercultural issues, for example, the tensions between the Hindu and Muslim political groups, and caste system within the Hindu society. How do we teach this aspect of Gandhi's creativity? Can we enable students to learn to become active citizens who can work through complex social problems? One conclusion my study arrived at is that instead of assimilating Gandhi's ideas and distilling them in the classroom, we need to learn from his radical thinking. My work sheds light on Gandhi's strategies, modes of thinking, behaviors, and beliefs as a citizen. Makiguchi and Gandhi did not provide a single, linear and reductive prescription for the needs of their respective societies, but instead, contended with the complexity of their respective social and educational contexts. Therefore, it must be argued that unlike what Rorty (1998) suggests, there are important lessons that can be learned for citizenship through studying such challenges and dilemmas that are faced by people and movements.

Further, as scholars such as Parekh (1989) have argued, the influence of Gandhi's religious views on his political understanding and action differ from Western political philosophies and can provide a new perspective on rights, duties, claims, interests, and obligations. For instance, as an outcome of his analysis Parekh (1997: 39–40) states: "that human beings were necessarily interdependent and formed an organic whole was another 'basic' truth about them according to Gandhi." Further Parekh (1997: 41) adds that since human beings were necessarily interdependent, they "could not degrade or brutalize others without also degrading and brutalizing themselves, or inflict psychic and moral damage on others without inflicting it on themselves as well" (also see Sharma 2008: 63–72).

So to address the second question raised earlier: "what does it mean to be an active citizen?," it can be said that apart from the attitude of a "can do" spirit of taking active engagement in one's community, the lives of Makiguchi and Gandhi suggest that an active citizen has a strong normative position which propels individual self-reflection and the propensity to effect a social change.

Taking political action based on one's beliefs also means that more often than not contradictions are likely to occur when personal values are placed in the real-world politics. Future research on other such thinkers, who were interested in the transformation of their own societies, should question the key contradictions and paradoxes that can be identified in a grounded or "situated" analysis of their respective ideas and value systems. During my work at the University of Nottingham, I tutored a module on critical and biographical analysis of texts in a master's in higher education course. Students undertaking project work on this module were concerned with a similar inquiry on the relevance of other thinkers like Paulo Freire and Immanuel Kant exploring key questions, such as: what were their personal histories?; who were they influenced by?; and in what context did they frame their ideas? These questions allow students to understand the context in which radical thinkers developed their ideas for action. Instead of teaching students that there is a single "correct way" or linear solution to combat social or political issues, these questions stimulate enquiry and imagination to understand the complexities involved in taking political action. In modern-day India often Gandhi is blamed for being a "hypocrite" (especially by those that have not even studied his work). Similarly, Makiguchi and his successors in Japan have sometimes encountered accusations, for instance, by "yellow journalism." This is a failure in part due to a lack of understanding of the fact that contradictions and paradoxes are inevitable when values engage with real-world politics. Therefore, a study of the lives of thinkers who were involved in their politics can enable readers to acquire critical understandings in the field of politics and the complexities of political processes in contemporary societies. This is necessary so that citizens can make a sound judgment and decisive action as political actors.

Tarc makes an important argument on the great emphasis being placed in recent years on developing active citizens within global citizenship education. Through his successive writings he states that, "In the Anglo-West, the global citizen aligns quite seamlessly with a middle-class neoliberal subjectivity in the form of a highly individuated, 'empowered' citizen who *chooses to*, using personal and private resources, chip in and 'make a difference'..." (Tarc 2011 in Tarc 2015: 36). On the other hand, Tarc suggests that in order to develop active global citizens in the twenty-first century, instead of the increasing demand for students to take action as change agents, there should first be a focus on learning issues related to global citizenship education with a critical approach within the classroom. This, in turn, can lead students to identify and take action based on their own volition on issues that are relevant to their schools and communities.

Module on Citizenship Education

As part of the Postgraduate Certificate Education (International) (PGCEi) course, at the University of Nottingham, the teaching unit, called "Makiguchi and Gandhi" was developed and has been available online since the beginning of 2011. The PGCEi course itself has more than 2500 students who have completed the program, with approximately 800 currently on course in several locations around the world.[4] The module is directed for teacher education. The "intended learning outcomes" are for the teachers to gain an awareness of the following:

- the educational ideas of two non-Western thinkers, Makiguchi and Gandhi;
- how Makiguchi and Ikeda's value-creating education can offer benefit in the context of the teacher's own classroom;
- the issues that arise in the teaching of values, such as Gandhi's non-violence; and
- a discussion on a qualitative approach to knowledge and values in citizenship education.

In this module, the students (who are mainly classroom teachers) engage with the original writings of Makiguchi and Gandhi, and activities allow them to develop their critical thinking and evaluate how the thinker's ideas can influence their own classroom practice. For some activities, videos are used from examples of teaching complex issues within citizenship education across the world.

In the first few sections, the learners are encouraged to read the life history of the thinkers, their educational theories, and the use of their ideas within selected schools. Through the step-by-step learning process, short written assignments are requested to facilitate the learners to reflect on how this study could impact upon their own classroom practice.

The learning content and activities within the module have been stylistically framed for students to use a comparative approach to study the ideas, practices, and influences of Makiguchi and Gandhi. This is with the aim to allow learners to note the similarities in Makiguchi and Gandhi's notions of truth and value, and also to identify similar aspects in their political movements and life history as dissident thinkers. For example, across time and cultural contexts, paradoxes emerge when personal values interact with real-world politics, as seen through the example of these thinkers and their successors.

The creativity of both thinkers is analyzed by contextualizing their contributions from their respective historical locales. The readings and activities review their specific influence on civic movements both at home and abroad, and the module concludes by discussing issues related to political or citizenship education for the twenty-first century.

The following are key points raised in this chapter that are also integrated into the design and content of the "Makiguchi and Gandhi" module.

1. The module allows learners to review and reflect on the contradictions and paradoxes that arise in taking action as a citizen through studying the lives of Makiguchi, Ikeda, and Gandhi.
2. This study is designed for teachers to have a critical and comprehensive understanding of how to teach related topics in the classroom. For instance, taking Gandhi's non-violent political action as an example, and with ample reading, teachers are asked to address the question, as to how and to what extent can the principles of non-violence be effectively taught within their classroom.

3. Through the selection of videos on best practices, teachers are also shown examples of teaching complex issues in citizenship education that can be relevant for classrooms across modern democratic nation states. An example is given from teachers in a selected school in the UK who share their challenges and experiences of teaching certain issues on human rights within Personal, social, health, and economic education (PSHE).[5]
4. Teachers are introduced to Makiguchi's value-creating theory that aimed at fostering people of creative talent who can contribute to personal and social good, as well as his proposals for teacher education. Assignments include discussion and reflection by teachers of any "good/successful teaching practice" which either they have adopted or could adopt in relation to enabling students to become more aware of local, social, or global issues.
5. For teachers to be better prepared to teach in a multicultural classroom context, this module offers a study of less widely known educational theories through a study of these selected Asian thinkers. (Several modules in the course engage with Western educational theorists—similar to many teachers' education courses worldwide.) In this module, teachers learn about Eastern theories of interdependence that Makiguchi, Ikeda, and Gandhi subscribed to and its impact on their respective education and politics (as developed through the arguments made earlier in this book).
6. The final section of this module revisits the role of knowledge and values in citizenship education. This is based on the arguments made in the previous chapter examining the concept of dialogue in teaching global citizenship education. In the module, the ontological paradigm underlying the perspective of the "self" and "other" is explored in key policy documents in the UK and within some of the debates on citizenship education in general. For example, various policies and documents suggest the need for more knowledge of the other. The rationale behind it seems to be that if we know more about the other person, community or society, we are likely to empathize more with them. However, as I demonstrate through examples, this may be a limited approach. In particular, because there are memories and politics associated with people and events even within contemporary politics, and just "knowing" about something does not enable us to truly understand a different perspective. An innovative approach, as

the final section of this module explores, is to take a qualitative and heuristic approach to knowledge and values, such as what may be found within Ikeda's philosophy of dialogue. The module emphasizes the need for an intervention that can bring together the self and other in dialogue to facilitate the individual self's growth and development within such interactions. In relation to this, key concepts in Ikeda's writings are studied (as explored in Chapter 4 of this book), including, "the oneness of self and environment" (*esho funi*), and "human revolution" (or individual change).

To summarize these concepts briefly, the relationship between the individual and her/his environment in Buddhism can be explained through the concept of *esho funi* in which the word *funi* essentially means "two but not two." This signifies the oneness or interdependence of the individual and environment.[6] According to the Buddhist view, that Makiguchi and Ikeda subscribed to, not only is the individual influenced and shaped by the environment, but also impacts upon it. Buddhism advocates taking positive action in one's daily life based on an attitudinal and behavioral change in the individual, which Makiguchi's successors Toda and Ikeda describe as "human revolution."[7] As also shown in the module, this is similar to the UNESCO goal of *learning to be* as one of the pillars of the Delors Report (1996) *Learning: the treasure within*.[8]

Practical activities related to this study include an assignment in which teachers are asked to share their views on how their classroom teaching can create better awareness of the individual learner's own environment and may help to build responsibility. In another assignment, teachers are shown a video on teaching citizenship education in a classroom in the US post 9-11. Based on this and the above theories, teachers are asked to think of practical lessons to make their teaching heuristic that can enable the learner to reflect upon one's own assumptions while engaging with global issues.

7. A qualitative approach to knowledge and values also means that instead of merely teaching values, institutions themselves should become models of change. The example is given of the Soka institutions in Japan that have been founded by Ikeda, as well as other successful examples of change made within the "untaught

> curriculum" and ethos of some schools that have adopted a "whole school approach" to the transformation of values. As demonstrated by these educational institutions (studied within this module), unless the schools themselves become models of change, that is, unless there is a specific way in which schools are able to actualize normative values within the taught and untaught curriculum, it will be hard to motivate students and enthuse them to perceive their responsibility as global citizens.

Some more specific strategies for teaching are offered in Chapter 7 of this book.

Conclusion and Moving Forward

Three key questions have been raised in this chapter in relation to citizenship education that have implications for the behavioral dimension of *learning to do* within global citizenship education. Who is a citizen? What does it mean to be an active citizen? And under what social, political, or educational scenario does a person become a citizen?

To reiterate, in response to the question, "who is a citizen?" a general agreement that we can reach given the different understandings for this term within different cultural contexts is that in modern democratic nation states a citizen is a resident with certain responsibilities, legal and political rights, including the right to vote. In engaging with "what it means to be an active citizen" through a study of Makiguchi and Gandhi, an aspect common to both their lives is that an active citizen has a strong normative position which propels individual self-reflection and the propensity to effect a social change. In this regard, schools need to engage with the personal values of learners. As argued earlier, "it is inadequate to 'politically' educate the learner within the closed brick walls of schools where in most cases the learner is expected to drop their 'identity, way of life, and its symbolic representations at the school gate'" (Sharma 2008: 155; also see Bernstein 1970: 345). For students to take a strong normative position, their values need to be engaged in within the classrooms.

The final question this chapter posed was "under what social, political or educational scenario does a person become a citizen?" A study of the lives of dissident thinkers shows that they were able to demonstrate active citizenship even within the challenges of an authoritarian or hostile environment. Although the context is very different in classrooms of modern day democratic nation states as also illustrated through various examples in this chapter, there are useful lessons we can learn from the lives and fates of these thinkers. Chapters 6 and 7 bring together the lessons from an engagement with these thinkers for the practice of global citizenship education.

Notes

1. Arguments made in this section were also a topic of consideration in Sharma (2012).
2. https://peoplesdecade2.wixsite.com/nuclear-abolition.
3. Non-violent resistance; a relentless search for truth; truth-force; holding on to truth. It is also the name of Gandhi's political movement.
4. As in Fall 2017. See https://www.nottingham.ac.uk/education/study/pgcei/index.aspx.
5. http://www.pshe-association.org.uk/content.aspx?CategoryID=335.
6. http://www.sgi-usa.org/memberresources/study/2016_essentials_part2/docs/eng/EssentialsExam2_p53_BuddhistConcepts-OnenessLifeEnvironment.pdf.
7. http://www.daisakuikeda.org/main/philos/buddhist/buddh-06.html.
8. http://www.unesco.org/new/en/education/themes/leading-the-international-agenda/rethinking-education/resources/.

References

Advisory Panel on Effectuation of Fundamental Duties of Citizens. (2001, July 6). *A consultation paper on the effectuation of fundamental duties of citizens.* New Delhi: National Commission to Review the Working of the Constitution.

Bernstein, B. (1970). Education cannot compensate for society. *New Society, 387,* 344–347.

Cappelle, G., Crippin, G., & Lundgren, U. (2011, September). *World citizenship education and teacher training in a global context: Canada, India, and South Africa.* London: CiCe Network. Retrieved from http://archive.londonmet.ac.uk/cice/fms/MRSite/Research/cice/pubs/citizenship/citizenship-08.pdf.

Delhi Historians' Group, J. N. U. (2001). *Communalisation of education: The history textbooks controversy.* New Delhi: Deluxe Printery.

Delors, J., et al. (1996). *Learning: The treasure within.* Paris: UNESCO.

Green, J. M. (2004). Participatory democracy: Movements, campaigns, and democratic living. *The Journal of Speculative Philosophy, 18*(1), 60–71.

Parekh, B. (1989). *Gandhi's political philosophy: A critical examination*. London: Macmillan.

Parekh, B. (1997). *Gandhi*. Oxford: Oxford University Press.

Rorty, R. (1998). *Achieving our country: Leftist thought in twentieth-century America*. Cambridge: Harvard University Press.

Sharma, N. (2008). *Makiguchi and Gandhi: Their educational relevance for the 21st century*. Lanham, MD: University Press of America and Rowman & Littlefield.

Sharma, N. (2012). Can we learn to become active citizens? In N. Palaiologou & G. Dietz (Eds.), *Mapping the broad field of intercultural/multicultural education worldwide: Towards the construction of the new citizen* (pp. 402–414). Newcastle: Cambridge Scholars Publishing.

Sharma, N. (2015). Can active citizenship be learned? Examining content and activities in a teacher's education module engaging with Gandhi and Makiguchi. In M. Mukherjee (Guest Ed.), *Indian education at the crossroads of postcoloniality, globalization and 21st century knowledge economy*, special issue II. *Policy Futures in Education, 13*(3), 328–341. Sage. http://dx.doi.org/10.1177/1478210315571215.

Tarc, P. (2011). How does "global citizenship education" construct its present? The crises of international education. In V. Andreotti & L. M. Menezes de Souza (Eds.), *Postcolonial perspectives in global citizenship education* (pp. 105–123). London: Routledge.

Tarc, P. (2015). What is the active in 21st century calls to develop "active global citizens?" Justice-oriented desires, active learning, neoliberal times. In J. Harshman, T. Augustine, & M. Merryfield (Eds.), *Research in global citizenship education* (pp. 35–58). Charlotte, NC: Information Age.

UNESCO, United Nations Educational Scientific and Cultural Organization. (2015). *Global citizenship education: Topics and learning objectives*. Paris: UNESCO.

PART II

Praxis

CHAPTER 6

The Practice of Value-Creating Global Citizenship Education

Abstract Based on a long-term study of Asian perspectives Sharma discusses the implications for *learning to live together* and brings together the various themes that were developed in the previous chapters for a practice of global citizenship education (GCE). The proposed six themes are, (i) a sense of interdependence, common humanity, and a global outlook; (ii) an awareness of climate change as planetary citizens; (iii) a commitment to reflective, dialogic, and transformative learning; (iv) a commitment to sustainable development through intercultural perspectives; (v) a belief in the value-creating capacity for social-self actualization; and (vi) an understanding of peace and non-violence as being central to the human rights agenda. These are relevant to K-12 teaching, and across various subject areas in higher education, within informal and non-formal education.

Keywords Global citizenship education · Learning to live together
Sustainable development · Planetary citizen · Soka education
Human rights

Introduction

This chapter offers suggestions to teach key issues that were identified in the preceding theoretical chapters. It is not intended as a guide to a curriculum on global citizenship education (GCE)—for which several

N. Sharma, *Value-Creating Global Citizenship Education*,
Palgrave Studies in Global Citizenship Education and Democracy,
https://doi.org/10.1007/978-3-319-78244-7_6

reference materials are available through Oxfam (2006a, 2015), The International Baccalaureate (Davy 2011), UNESCO (2014, 2015), UNICEF (2013), and other work that provide a detailed outline of issues concerning GCE and how to teach it as a course from the kindergarten to high school, such as, *Empowering global citizens—A world course* (Reimers et al. 2016).

Themes and approaches are developed in this chapter for a global content offering perspectives from the study of non-Western thinkers that can be infused or incorporated within formal, non-formal, and informal education settings. These pedagogical approaches can be delivered as an integral part of an existing subject. For example, in schools within civics or citizenship education, social studies, social/environmental studies, health education; and across disciplines in higher education including within programs that integrate sustainability issues and social responsibility.

The discussions in this chapter are aimed at initial and in-service teachers, teacher educators, as well as those engaged with developing curriculum within undergraduate and masters' programs. It also addresses administrators, paraprofessionals, policy makers and all those who are interested in promoting GCE in schools, higher education institutions, civil society organizations and other forums that support the education of youth as citizens of the twenty-first century.

Developing a Pedagogical Framework for Value-Creating Global Citizenship Education

Within GCE it is often challenging to prescribe what needs to be taught across diverse nation states, for example, where there are different legal rights and responsibilities. GCE should therefore be regarded as an ethos, a framework to develop the knowledge, skills, values, attitudes, and behaviors that are required to respond to global issues that affect people's lives locally (see Tarozzi and Torres 2016: 14–16). Pedagogical approaches discussed in this chapter propose a framework that is based on alternative paradigms and perspectives in GCE that were discussed in the previous chapters.

To recapitulate, non-Western examples can challenge a re-examination of research and praxis in GCE (entrenched in a Western paradigm). Two important outcomes can be generated through a study of the selected Asian thinkers. First, their perspectives although situated in non-Western historical contexts were also influenced by the West. A study of their ideas can make important contributions to the existing discourse on consciousness and competencies within GCE. The second is that the examples of movements that motivate people to take positive action within their respective societies are embedded with learning that can inform classroom practice in GCE. As an example, a study of the *satyagraha* movement demonstrates that normative values like non-violence can effectively engage through creative processes even within political realities (Sharma 2008). Further, it is also important to recognize that contradictions and paradoxes arise as values engage with politics. This needs to be part of the central discourse and praxis on GCE . Recent studies such as by Davies (2006) encourage an engagement with controversial issues in teaching citizenship that can enhance criticality as has also been stressed in Andreotti's (2006) seminal proposal for a critical global citizenship:

> In this sense, critical literacy is not about 'unveiling' the 'truth' for the learners, but about providing the space for them to reflect on their context and their own and others' epistemological and ontological assumptions: how we came to think/be/feel/act the way we do and the implications of our systems of belief in local/global terms in relation to power, social relationships and the distribution of labour and resources.
>
> (Andreotti 2006: 49)

The disposition and agenda of GCE that the preceding theoretical chapters promote are:

1. criticality for social justice, and
2. value creation for social-self actualization.

These are regarded here as being central to a value-creating education framework for GCE. It includes the skills of criticality for social justice, knowledge that is dialogic and socio-emotional behavior that is transformative for social-self actualization. To explain, Makiguchi, Gandhi, Ikeda, and others in their lineage across time and place have adopted a strong normative position in engaging with issues on social justice within their own particularities and in an attempt to create positive change at individual and social levels. Their examples have important lessons for fostering youth as citizens through education within schools and other organizations of learning. The discussions in this chapter make suggestions to use their examples within praxis while engaging with issues that are considered as being relevant to the United Nations Educational Scientific and Cultural Organization (UNESCO) led practice of GCE. This framework should not be treated as a new subject for teaching, but rather, echoing Annette Scheunpflug's (2011) proposals for global learning as Bourn (2014: 16) describes, it is "a guiding principle defined by thematic issues...and competencies that need to be acquired to live in a global society." These competencies include the ability to "understand and critically reflect global interdependencies, own values and attitudes, develop own positions and perspectives, see options, capability to make choices, to participate in communication and decisions within a global context" (Scheunpflug 2011: 33–34 in Bourn 2014: 16).

Teaching around these guiding principles, competencies, and possibilities is open to the creativity of the teacher that can be developed within particularities and in interactions with the needs of the student. The theoretical underpinnings of the pedagogy of the teacher and the curriculum developers have an effect on the practice within classrooms. Introducing themes that emerge from a study of the selected Asian thinkers to the discourse and practice of GCE can contribute to the development of a multicultural curriculum. Further, the examples of these dissidents advocate the importance of developing criticality to respond to structural inequities and inequalities at local and global levels.

In contrast to a Western liberal-individualistic framework for GCE, a value-creating education framework at the most basic level subscribes to a non-dualistic view of life that promotes a unity of consciousness aimed at enhancing relationships in education (see Goulah and Ito 2012; Ikegami and Rivalland 2016; Nagashima 2016; Takazawa 2016). Its central concern is to perceive, acknowledge, and remove "the arrow of a discriminatory consciousness, an unreasoning emphasis on difference... piercing the hearts of the people" (Ikeda 1993: 2, as elaborated on in Chapter 4). A shift in paradigm and perspectives as argued earlier, will have a significant bearing on the praxis and the three domains of learning within the GCE conceptual dimensions of UNESCO—the cognitive, socio-emotional, and behavioral (UNESCO 2015: 14–15). These correspond to the four pillars of learning described in the UNESCO (2001) report *Learning: The treasure within*, that are, learning to know, to do, to be and to live together. For example, an acknowledgement of one's common humanity would give emphasis to perceiving the divisiveness and alienation that is present within modern societies. That is, it would place a strong emphasis within the curriculum to tackle stereotyping and foster the socio-emotional capacity of compassion toward all inhabitants of the earth whilst also recognizing the nature and forms of power structures in an increasingly globalized world and the unseen perpetuation of colonial perspectives. The behavioral response to solve global issues would be rooted in a non-dualistic belief system that through an intuitive examination of the depth of human life subscribes to the view that an attitudinal change within each person can impact upon their environment (see Ikeda 2003: 106). The educational environment will be developed to foster meaningful life-to-life connections among people—between students and teachers, schools and communities, and so on.

The proposed framework covers six themes within the practice of value-creating GCE that aim to promote the necessary knowledge, skills, values, and attitudes to enable learners to develop:

- **A Sense of Interdependence, Common Humanity, and a Global Outlook**: that explores existential questions including that from non-Western perspectives; while also challenging colonial perspectives.
- **An Awareness of Climate Change as Planetary Citizens**: that acknowledges that climate change is real; develops reverence for nature; a wonder and appreciation for life as creative coexistence; and mandates an urgent action and concern for the welfare of the planet by the citizens of the earth.
- **A Commitment to Reflective, Dialogic, and Transformative Learning**: that prioritizes not just a quantitative approach to acquiring more knowledge about others but a qualitative one that facilitates the development of the learner's own values and attitudes through dialogic processes.
- **A Commitment to Sustainable Development through Intercultural Perspectives**: that engages with particularities and specificities of the local while also connecting with global issues; and the integration of lessons from history on the normative and creative use of values across societies such that a study of these dissidents and their movements can promote.
- **A Belief in the Value-Creating Capacity for Social-Self Actualization**: that can approach issues concerned with social justice, gender, and equity through developing the value-creating capacity of the learner to contribute to individual benefit and social good.

- **An Understanding of Peace and Non-Violence as being Central to the Human Rights Agenda**: that builds character through a critical engagement with studies on the patterns of living of people and communities across Western/non-Western diasporas that are based on peace and non-violence.

Figure 6.1 illustrates the proposed framework based on a value-creating paradigm for global citizenship education.

Fig. 6.1 Framework for value-creating global citizenship education

Themes Within the Practice of Value-Creating Global Citizenship Education

This section elaborates on the above themes developed from the preceding research chapters. The structure for this section is informed by the framework used in a study on *The theory and practice of global learning* by Bourn (2014). An engagement with these themes should take place within the context of the previous discussions that can stimulate creativity and imagination of alternative perspectives and possibilities within teaching and learning. Within each theme a brief description is provided that challenges epistemic assumptions and offers suggestions for practice. Overall these themes are designed to support the learner's happiness, well-being, and the development of the capacity to create value.

A Sense of Interdependence, Common Humanity, and a Global Outlook

Key Points
Developing a sense of interdependence, common humanity, and a global outlook from a value-creating global citizenship perspective should:

- explore existential questions including that from non-Western perspectives; and
- challenge colonial perspectives.

Challenging Assumptions
The promotion of a "common humanity" is an overarching theme within UNESCO's GCE that encourages praxis centered on empathizing with and taking action to remove poverty and inequality.[1] Charity and advocacy have therefore often been a big part of taking action as a global citizen. Whilst these are important, as Andreotti (2006) suggests, these actions would not necessarily challenge the students' ignorance of the structural roots of inequalities and inequities which are often a result of colonial pasts. She advocates that while a "soft" approach of developing a moral concern is appropriate, it must be combined with a "hard" approach that enables learners to become "critically literate" or they might end up perpetuating the same issues that cause the widening gaps related to poverty, inequality, and inequity at various levels.

Within the various calls for developing a sense of interdependence, common humanity, and a global outlook, by inviting non-Western perspectives that are similar to or distinct from the conversations helps to challenge presumptions based on neoliberal perspectives. As an example, a core concept within Buddhist humanism is the understanding of *jihi* or compassion that emerges from the Indian terminologies of *metta* and *karuna*, which is a combination of "true friendship," "unconditional love," and "empathy" (see glossary for *jihi*, *metta*, and *karuna*). That which draws us to the world of the other as viewed through this Asian perspective includes empathy (often advocated in praxis within GCE) but also incorporates the aspect of friendship. A compassionate disposition creates a mutual and equal relationship. Ikeda (2008) suggests compassion as being an essential element of global citizenship that resonates with the Sanskrit phrase *Vasudhaiva Kutumbakam*—the whole world is one family.

Suggestions for Practice

These might seem as philosophical narratives but they are imperative to engage with in the classroom starting from stories in pre-K classrooms to a robust discussion of non-Western philosophical, existential, and ontological understandings in higher education.

The discourse and practice of GCE should generate some of these philosophical discussions that enable students to understand the expansiveness of their own lives from a cosmological point of view and promote a deeper ontological understanding of the interdependence of life (as outlined in the previous chapters). The practice of teaching GCE can be informed by a wider raft of pedagogical contributions within specific subject areas.

This theme engages with the values of friendship, empathy, and compassion. Outside of the curriculum this theme supports the benefits from study abroad and international exchange programs but emphasizes the need to integrate opportunities that can enhance students' spectrum of meaningful engagements within their local communities. This is necessary to develop empathy and compassion at a global level. One of Ikeda's criteria for global citizenship is the "compassion to maintain an imaginative empathy that reaches beyond one's immediate surroundings and extends to those suffering in distant places" (Ikeda 2008: 444). A similar intent can be found in Gandhi's talisman, which reads,

> Whenever you are in doubt, or when the self becomes too much with you, apply the following test. Recall the face of the poorest and the weakest (wo)man who you may have seen, and ask yourself if the step you contemplate is going to be of any use to him (or her). Will s/he gain anything by it? Will it restore him (or her) ... Then you will find your doubts and ... self melting away.
>
> (Fischer 1983: 316)

"A soft approach" in emphasizing a moral concern is a good starting point (Andreotti 2006). However, lessons developed on thinkers like Gandhi should also be used to showcase examples of creativity used to develop just and equitable communities while displacing power structures that cause inequalities (such as discussed in Chapter 2). It is important to note that often in lessons on Gandhi there is a great deal of emphasis on Gandhi the moral leader, and less about the radical Gandhi or the creative Gandhi.

An Awareness of Climate Change as Planetary Citizens

Key Points
Generating an awareness of climate change is based on:

- an acknowledgement that climate change is real;
- develops a reverence for nature;
- a wonder and appreciation for life as creative coexistence; and
- mandates an urgent action and concern by the citizens of the earth.

Challenging Assumptions
As mentioned in the preceding chapters, one of the influences of the scientific-industrial revolution originating from the West is a mechanistic and reductionist view of life. On the other hand, a non-dualistic view perceives the dynamic relationship between the self and the natural/social environment as being fluid and in a constant state of creative engagement and coexistence (see Chapter 4 for further details). While the wisdom and energy to take action in tackling climate change are perceived here as being important, it should also be with an attitude of reverence for life as suggested in the Earth Charter that resonates with Makiguchi's sentiments described in his work *Jinsei chirigaku* or the Geography of Human Life (Makiguchi 1983).

It's worth noting that the success of the Earth Charter and its adoption by several schools is not only that it offers a comprehensive overview as an invaluable educational resource, but that, as Ikeda points out, "the manner in which this 'people's charter' was drafted is significant…in the drafting process, efforts were made to incorporate the essential wisdom of cultures and traditions from all regions of Earth" (Ikeda 2002). In his Columbia Speech, Ikeda proposes as an essential element of a global citizen "the wisdom to perceive the interconnectedness of all life and living" (Ikeda 2008: 444). This wisdom, Ikeda notes is a "living wisdom" that can be learned from various cultural traditions that appreciate the unity and connectedness of life, such as, the Desana people of the Amazon and the Iroquois people of North America" (Ikeda 2002). One of the consequences of similar worldviews has lead some nations states, including Ireland and India, to give constitutional rights to trees and rivers as being sacred.

Suggestions for Practice
Climate change is a reality that still does not have universal consensus (the US withdrawing from the Paris Agreement on climate change in 2017 is a startling example). The first step is to combat this ignorance within issues related to GCE. It is to enable an understanding and develop a commitment toward tackling climate change as outlined by UNESCO's Education for Sustainable Development (ESD) program. Moving beyond a cognitive approach, education for climate change should create a learning environment that can cause a socio-emotional response in students to develop a reverence for nature, and care and responsibility as citizens of this planet. Further, a critical understanding is required of the causal relationship between human strife and suffering, and the destruction of natural and other forms of life (the Syrian crises and conflicts in the Middle East are among such examples).

As a starting point the following references can be used to approach these issues from a value-creating perspective: Henderson and Ikeda's (2004) dialogue *Planetary citizens*; Makiguchi's (1983) book, *The Geography of Human Life* (Bethel 2002 for an edited English translation; also see Bethel 2000; Takeuchi 2004), the *Earth charter initiative*[2] (also see Rockefeller 2015), and UNESCO's climate change education and awareness initiatives.[3]

A Commitment to Reflective, Dialogic, and Transformative Learning

Key Points
A commitment to a reflective, dialogic, and transformative approach needs to be located within the processes of learning designed to:

- create a shift from the emphasis on a quantitative approach of acquiring more knowledge about others to a qualitative one in which the learner experiences trust, empathy, and friendship through the learning process; and
- that can ensure the development of the learner's own values and attitudes through such dialogic processes (as explained through examples in Chapter 4).

Challenging Assumptions
Various studies on promoting reflective, dialogic, and transformative experiences within the global dimension of learning include contributions by Bourn (2014: 28–30), Kumar (2008), and Scheunpflug (2012). In this work Chapter 4 was positioned to develop a holistic approach to dialogue through the study of non-Western perspectives, and the integration of dialogic processes within the taught and untaught curriculum.

Suggestions for Practice
The process of value-creating education is to internalize dialogue generated through being inspired by others/nature/the universe. The process of dialogue should start from the learner's immediate environment, at home with the family, within the class and school, and through an engagement in the community.

Chapter 4 provides a more detailed engagement with this theme. As mentioned, it is to go beyond dialogue as verbal communication to reimagining how dialogic processes can be integrated into learning and teaching for global citizenship, including the representation of the "other" within the curriculum. As an example, UNESCO has been working on textbook development issues since its inception in 1945 as part of its fundamental mandate to "build peace in the minds of men and women" (see UNESCO 2017). It has aimed at "the removal of content leading to negative stereotyping of the 'other,' narrow nationalism, and the glorification of war" (UNESCO 2017: 7). Further, in engaging with religion, gender, and culture, "more recent initiatives on textbooks and learning materials have broadened to include considerations of the role of education in promoting human rights and ending discrimination in all of its forms" (ibid.). It is imperative here that the UNESCO agenda of *learning to live together* (Delors 1996) should also be revisited from a *dharmic* philosophical perspective, being mindful of the role of development that it can promote through internalizing dialogue with the "other" as discussed in the theoretical chapters.

A Commitment to Sustainable Development Through Intercultural Perspectives

Key Points
A commitment to sustainable development through intercultural perspectives is based on:

- the engagement with particularities and specificities of the local;
- while also engaging with global lessons on the normative and creative use of values within socio-political affairs across societies such that a study of creative dissidents and their movements can promote;
- this theme has a strong focus on intercultural education within the Incheon Declaration and Framework for Action for the implementation of UNESCO's Sustainable Development Goal (SDG) 4 (UNESCO 2016).

Challenging Assumptions
Following up from the arguments in Chapter 3, the practice of GCE can work best within a curriculum that represents the knowledge of a varied group of people. As mentioned, this proposal follows from a previous co-authored paper on the topic of sustainable development in higher education, in which it was suggested that whereas sustainable development has often been associated with environmental concerns (Morris 2008), an approach to issues of sustainability from an intercultural perspective can draw from diverse wisdom and knowledge that is in line with UNESCO's aims for ESD (Gundara and Sharma 2010).

Also, developing criticality in knowledge through post-structural lenses is important. It goes beyond the development of a critical approach, such as suggested by Oxfam (2006a). It is the recognition of the structural roots of power and the inequalities and inequities created through economic, social, and political forces (see Bourn 2014: 25–26). It requires, as in the earlier citation from Andreotti (2006: 49), an engagement with intercultural perspectives to provide the space for learners "to reflect on their context and their own and others' epistemological and ontological assumptions: how we came to think/be/feel/act the way we do and the implications of our systems of belief in local/global terms in relation to power, social relationships and the distribution of labour and resources."

Toward this the first step in education for global citizenship is to engage with the values of the learner so as to enable them to develop their own identities in a positive way. Here especially relevant is a recent study by Dill (2013) on selected religious and public schools that engage with particularities in GCE instead of flattening out differences. An example given is that of Muslim young women respondents who as Dill describes state that, "the particulars of their religious faith serve as a source for their commitment to more universal themes of global citizenship" (Dill 2013: 131). This is similar to Gandhi. As mentioned in my previous study, "as Gandhi claimed, being a 'good' Hindu did not lead him to the Himalayas, but forced him to contend with the issues within the Indian society and politics" (Sharma 2008: 129). Also as discussed in Chapter 2, Gandhi's Indian, Gujarati, Hindu background and diasporic experiences have particular relevance to the socially diverse polity of present-day democratic nation states. This is especially relevant because it is indicative of the various layers of identities of the diaspora which influenced him.

Suggestions for Practice

A study of thinkers like Gandhi, Makiguchi, and Ikeda can shed light on their engagement with particularities, values, and beliefs that lead to their strategies and action to create positive change and sustainable communities within their respective geographical locales.

Further, as found in the previous research chapters in this book that examined the use and relevance of these thinkers, there are contradictions and paradoxes that arise when ideas and values engage with political realities. As an outcome, the study proposed that students need to be equipped with critical understandings of the political implications of living together in the twenty-first century. Other recent studies and teaching guides, including by Davies (2006) and Oxfam (2006b) encourage an engagement with controversial issues in teaching global citizenship (also see Andreotti and Warwick 2007).

A more recent and comprehensive study was conducted by Hess and McAvoy (2015) through a longitudinal survey and discussions with 35 teachers and their students on teaching controversial political issues from the year 2005 to 2009. Defining their research position they state,

> We argue that schools are, and ought to be, political sites. In this context, we use the term "political" as it applies to the role of citizens within a democracy: *We are being political when we are democratically making decisions about questions that ask, "How should we live together?"* By extension, the *political classroom* is one that helps students develop their ability to deliberate political questions. When teachers engage students in discussions about what rules ought to be adopted by a class, they are teaching them to think politically. Similarly, when teachers ask students to research and discuss a current public controversy, such as, "Should same-sex marriage be legally recognized?," they are engaging in politics.
>
> (Hess and McAvoy 2015: 4)

Hess and McAvoy recommend that in encouraging such discussions, schools should not be *partisan* institutions, particularly that public schools should not favor a particular political party. While at the same time the outcome from their study also confirms my position that the UNESCO agenda of *learning to live together* (Delors et al. 1996) has political implications. UNESCO's aims of Intercultural Education highlights this agenda as its core aim (UNESCO 2006). A more robust engagement with this agenda should be made through the proposals under this theme within the policy and praxis on GCE.

Hess and McAvoy's work makes useful references to teach controversial issues on GCE within the classroom as they examine the "political education paradox" of the contrast between "the need to provide students with a nonpartisan political education on the one hand with the need to prepare them to participate in the actual, highly partisan political community on the other" (Hess and McAvoy 2015: 4). The authors provide examples of how teachers can navigate ethical questions within the classroom which as they state are "unusual political spaces" (ibid.: 6). Suggestions offered are in a way that is fair, age appropriate, and culturally sensitive, and that prepares students for democratic life. As well as, their recommendations encourage teachers to combat "the fear of parental and public backlash" (ibid.) by providing examples of how they can engage students in political deliberation and discussion. These and other such useful materials are available for teachers, parents, school administrators, and intermediary organizations that can be used as a guiding framework to engage with the creative use of values in politics, such as that of *ahimsa* or non-violence in the movement of *satyagraha*, and the goal of world peace within the Soka movement.

A Belief in the Value-Creating Capacity for Social-Self Actualization

Key Points

The final two themes within a value-creating framework for GCE are related to the development of the character through education. The educational ideas of Makiguchi and Ikeda indicate that inherent within human life is the capacity to create value for oneself and others under any circumstances, and that this capacity should be developed through education. As an outcome of this continued process of engaging in the act of value creation for social-self actualization character is formed.

Challenging Assumptions

Value creation and not value consumption is being proposed within this framework. It is not to teach values but enable the learner to develop the inherent capacity they each possess to build wisdom from exercising knowledge in action, and to use that wisdom for the betterment of oneself and society. It is also to foster tenacity, perseverance and generate an understanding of the inherent creative potential within human life to transform difficulties and challenges into opportunities.

Suggestions for Practice

In approaching issues concerned with social justice, gender, and other forms of disparities, and to bring about equality and equity there is a need to develop the value-creating capacity of the learner so that they can contribute to individual benefit and social good. The first step for this at an institutional level is to set the agenda of building a mission statement that asks what is the purpose of cultivating intellect. The second step is to enable the transformation of knowledge to wisdom through providing opportunities to engage with issues on social justice through experience and action within one's school and local community. Guiding questions should include not only what impact can the learner create for the benefit of others, but also how they can develop their own capacity, that is, what knowledge, skills, values, and attitudes have they acquired through working with others? The main outcome from an engagement with issues on social justice should be to foster learners as agents of social transformation but with the dual goal of how that transformation has developed their own lives in terms of tapping into their inner resources such as wisdom, courage, and compassion.

An Understanding of Peace and Non-violence as Being Central to the Human Rights Agenda

Key Points

This theme stems from Gandhi's proposals for the development of character through education. It suggests building character through a critical engagement with studies on the patterns of living of people and communities across Western/non-Western diasporas that are based on peace and non-violence.

Challenging Assumptions

Several recommendations are made by UNESCO under the peace and human rights agenda that includes, preventing violent extremism through education, and education about the holocaust.[4] Within these agendas, what is meant by power is also a key theme that needs to be part of this process of learning. As Bourn points out, "Power is complex and cannot be seen in terms of traditional colonial powers versus colonies. Globalisation has transformed many of the social, cultural, political and economic relationships that exist around the world" (Bourn 2014: 26). As viewed from Eastern ontological lenses the good and evil divide that is "rooted in a worldview of fixed categories of good and evil" (Ikeda 2014: 15), that has often been used as the rationale to fight wars among nations becomes inconsequential in light of the existential perspective based on a non-dualistic view of good and evil. Both good and evil are seen to be part of every individual, society, and nation. In essence, evil is that which alienates people and destroys life, and good is that which brings people together and upholds the sanctity and dignity of life. Peace and non-violence are in this way central to the human rights agenda.

Also, and in practical terms, as echoed in the Universal Declaration of Human Rights, children have a right to receive education and express themselves in a safe space where the rights of the girl child across many schools and communities deserve more attention. At a micro level each child has a right to education within schools that are committed to tackling bullying and violence. At the macro level of the local and global communities they have a right to a world without the threat of poverty, war, and nuclear weapons.[5]

Suggestions for Practice

This theme poses many curricular challenges which are nevertheless considered as being pertinent to a value-creating framework for GCE.

A critical understanding of the complex and changing dimensions of power in a post-colonial world are central to the praxis of GCE. As an example, the discussions on the "second Gandhi" in Chapter 5 are relevant to this theme. As argued, instead of assimilating Gandhi's ideas and distilling it in the classroom, we need to learn from his radical thinking. That is, to shed light on Gandhi's strategies, behaviors, and beliefs as a citizen. Makiguchi, Gandhi, Ikeda, and similar creative thinkers have not provided a single, linear and reductive prescription for the needs of their respective societies, but instead, contended with the complexity of their respective social and educational contexts.

A study of the use and misuse of Gandhi within Indian history textbooks in early twenty-first century also allows educators to challenge the agendas that dictate national and local educational policies, curriculum theorizing and development. For example, as examined in Chapters 2 and 5, Gandhi and the value of non-violence have been treated in different ways under changing political regimes even within the education of democratic nation states.

Issues and Concerns for Teachers to Consider

Agency and Trust

Gebert and Joffee's (2007) research on the various observational studies conducted on the practice of value-creating education concludes with the following remarks.

> From these brief accounts, it can be seen that Soka education stresses the power of the individual teacher to challenge educational difficulties through his or her personal efforts. In each of these cases, much as in the example set by Makiguchi, teachers personally undertook difficult challenges and created a pathway to learning and happiness by dint of personal courageous action.
>
> (Gebert and Joffee 2007: 81)

The practice of a value-creating education framework places a great emphasis on the role of the educator. Further, through my work on the Soka Schools in Japan (Sharma 2008) I find that there is a strong impact of the institutional ethos on the sense of trust experienced by all students in the contributions that they can make as "global citizens" to the local community and the wider world. I refer to this as the "existing but untaught curriculum" that essentially applies to all Soka educational institutions (Fig. 6.2).

In a value-creating framework for GCE trust in the individual's capacity for social-self actualization becomes a key factor for success. The process of engaging with the learners should start with (1) an engagement with their aspirations, (2) support for their efforts to fulfill their responsibilities and potential for social-self actualization, (3) that can lead to developing their conviction in themselves as global citizens, and (4) the courage to take action supported by their conviction, (5) resulting in creativity, (6) that leads to developing their hope to pursue their dreams.

Building Relations

Davies' (2006) study finds several constraints stated by teachers in the practice of GCE, including a curriculum overload, resources, time, and confidence. In addition, as a UNESCO study notes, there are several tensions that arise in teaching GCE.[6] Among these and others that are particularly relevant when adopting a value-creating framework within a dominant individualistic-liberal paradigm are the tensions that arise between

- how to promote universality versus particularity;
- how to give agency to the individual but not get trapped in promoting individualism;
- how to foster relationships;
- how to support value creation for social-self actualization?

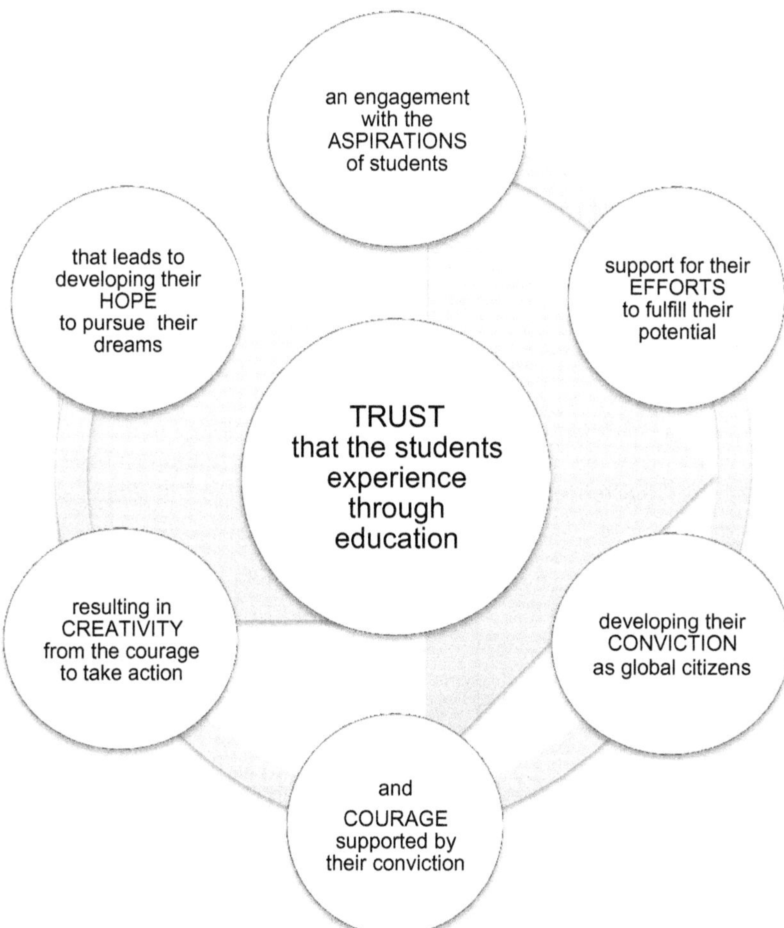

Fig. 6.2 Ikeda's humanistic education within the Soka educational institutions (adapted from Ikeda 2016)

As discussed through the study of the three selected thinkers, a trusting relationship between the learner and other students/the educator/institution/community are indispensable to the practice of value-creating education. The engagement of the learner with the educational material is also a key factor. Developing the discussion on Makiguchi's educational pedagogy in Chapter 2, Figs. 6.3 and 6.4 explain the process through which value can be created in education.

First, the individual must be able to objectively view the truth or fact for what it is. And then, make a subjective analysis of the best way to create value within that reality. As mentioned, Makiguchi states that value can be created in our *relationship* with an object. The object can be a material object or a person, a sentient or insentient being. Value creation is a two-step process of:

1. objectively recognizing the sentient or insentient object, or fact for what it is, and then
2. subjectively evaluating it to create value.

According to Makiguchi, one of the aims of education is to develop a relationship between the learner and the learning content. Instead of transferring "piecemeal merchandizing of information," teachers should

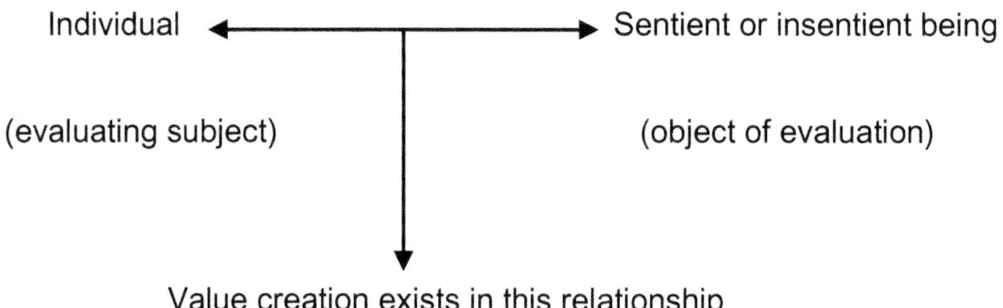

Fig. 6.3 The process of value creation in life

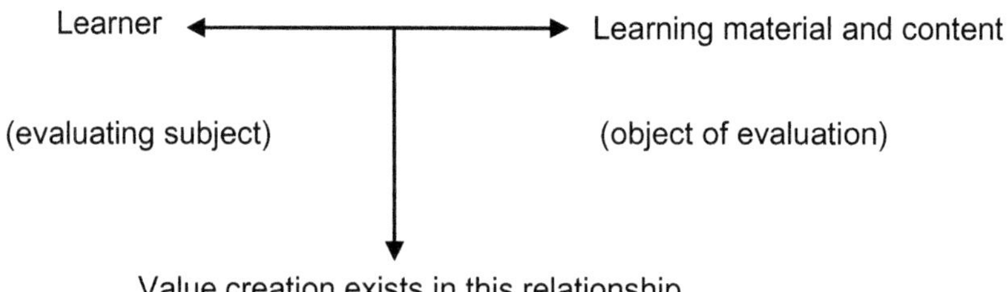

Fig. 6.4 The process of value creation in education

build engagement between the learner and their learning material. While it was common practice to transfer or cram knowledge into the minds of children during his time, Makiguchi aimed to facilitate inquiry and the process of learning (Bethel 1989: 168).

Further, in stressing the importance of distinguishing between cognition and evaluation within classroom teaching, Makiguchi gives the following example,

> Suppose a student asks his teacher, "What does this mean?" and the teacher snaps back the reprimand, "What do you mean? Don't you understand that yet?" The teacher obviously confuses evaluation with cognition. The student did not ask for an evaluation of his ability; he was asking for information or for instruction on a point he did not understand.... Regrettably, similar leaps of judgement past the facts are encountered at every level of society – in government, in business, and in the home.
>
> (Bethel 1989: 62–63)

The practice of value-creating education in global citizenship can be effectively carried out when the ethos of the institution, the curriculum, and teaching practices are dialogic and transformative. It embraces the home-school-community continuum in which the individual learner lives her/his life is where value creation can be practiced.

Another important contribution of the process of value creation is to enable students to distinguish between an "emergent truth" versus an "objective truth." For example, it is crucial that students recognize objective truth like climate change. As the scientist Neil de Grasse Tyson emphasizes, when two politicians are arguing about an issue that is a scientific truth, it is the beginning of the end of an informed democracy (King 2017). Chapter 7 uses critical textual analysis as an example of a method that can enable students to develop criticality for social justice. Some examples of how students can also create value within the given threats posed by climate change is to engage in a study of clean energy and resilience, that members of the academic scientific community like Katherine Hayhoe are engaged in developing.[7] The teacher's role is indispensable to open up the minds and develop the creativity of the protagonists of the twenty-first century.

Conclusion and Moving Forward

This chapter brings together the various discussions in the previous chapters for a practice of GCE. To recapitulate, Chapter 2 engaged with the Asian thinkers' core ideas, strategies, behaviors, and beliefs as active protagonists in their respective countries. Chapter 3 contributed to the cognitive dimension of *learning to know*. It engaged in a discussion on what should be part of the learning experience. For example, it was argued that the curriculum should be non-centric and represent intercultural perspectives. Also, the focus within GCE needs to expand from individual empowerment to an emphasis on a collective effort to create value for self and others. Chapter 4 discussed issues related to the socio-emotional dimension of *learning to be* from Asian perspectives that develop a sense of interdependence and common humanity, and promote dialogic, reflective, and transformative learning experiences. Chapter 5 explored the behavioral dimension of *learning to do* involving a critical analysis of what it means to be an active citizen. For instance, a study of these thinkers shows that there are political implications of taking action based on values, such as, peace and non-violence. This chapter visited the implications for *learning to live together*, bringing together the discussions on the various interrelated domains of global citizenship (cognitive, socio-emotional, and behavioral) to develop themes that emerge from the previous theoretical chapters for a practice of GCE (with the addition of climate change). The following six themes were proposed in this chapter, (i) a sense of interdependence, common humanity, and a global outlook; (ii) an awareness of climate change as planetary citizens; (iii) a commitment to reflective, dialogic, and transformative learning; (iv) a commitment to sustainable development through intercultural perspectives; (v) a belief in the value-creating capacity for social-self actualization; and (vi) an understanding of peace and non-violence as being central to the human rights agenda.

In conclusion, it is suggested that the research on value-creating GCE should start with an investigation of the dominant as well as alternative paradigms and perspectives. However, in praxis we need to start from possibilities, that is, to begin with a belief in the learner's unlimited potential.

A value-creating framework for GCE necessitates taking steps toward moving the educational decision-making into the hands of those who are on the front lines of education. The teacher is regarded as the most important educational environment for the learner (including the voice, smile, and the disposition of the teacher). This framework is based on the worldview that even though technology can be used to facilitate learning, only humans can truly foster other humans. It subscribes to a student-centered education; the limitless potential within each learner; the importance of encouraging students so that they can develop the knowledge, skills, values, and attitudes required to contribute to their own happiness as well as the welfare of others. The overarching goal of education and an educational institution's true worth are consequently determined by the success of its graduates' happiness, health, and ability to create value for self and others.

Notes

1. http://en.unesco.org/gced.
2. http://earthcharter.org/discover/the-earth-charter/.
3. http://en.unesco.org/themes/addressing-climate-change/climate-change-education-and-awareness.
4. http://en.unesco.org/gced.
5. The practice of global citizenship education should seriously engage with the work being done by the anti-nuclear weapons group, ICAN, that won the Nobel Peace Prize in 2017. See http://www.icanw.org/.
6. http://unesdoc.unesco.org/images/0022/002241/224115E.pdf.
7. http://katharinehayhoe.com/wp2016/blog/.

References

Andreotti, V. (2006). Soft versus critical global citizenship education. *Policy & Practice: A Development Education Review*, *3*(Autumn), 40–51.

Andreotti, V., & Warwick, P. (2007). *Engaging students with controversial issues through a dialogue based approach*. Published online by Citized. Retrieved from http://www.citized.info/?r_menu=res&strand=3.

Bethel, D. M. (Ed.). (1989). *Education for creative living: Ideas and proposals of Tsunesaburo Makiguchi*. Ames: Iowa State University Press.

Bethel, D. M. (2000). The legacy of Tsunesaburo Makiguchi: Value creating education and global citizenship. In D. Machacek & B. Wilson (Eds.), *Global citizens: The Soka Gakkai Buddhist movement in the world* (pp. 42–66). Oxford: Oxford University Press.

Bethel, D. M. (Ed.). (2002). *The geography of human life*. San Francisco: Caddo Gap Press.

Bourn, D. (2014). *The theory and practice of global learning* (Research Paper No. 11 for the Global Learning Programme). London: Development Education Research Center, Institute of Education, Global Learning Programme.

Davies, L. (2006). Global citizenship: Abstraction or framework for action? *Educational Review, 58*(1), 5–25.

Davy, I. (2011). *Learners without borders: A curriculum for global citizenship*. International Baccalaureate Organization. Retrieved from http://repository.smsd.org/docs/Public/Education/IB/RS5JNB5QAG/A-CURRICULUM-FOR-GLOBAL-CITIZENSHIP-en.pdf.

Delors, J., et al. (1996). *Learning: The treasure within*. Paris: UNESCO.

Dill, J. S. (2013). *The longings and limits of global citizenship education: The modern pedagogy of schooling in a cosmopolitan age*. New York: Routledge.

Fischer, L. (1983). *The essential Gandhi: His life, word and ideas. An anthology*. New York: Vintage Books.

Gebert, A., & Joffee M. (2007). Value creation as the aim of education: Tsunesaburo Makiguchi and Soka education. In D. T. Hansen (Ed.), *Ethical visions in education: Philosophies in practice* (pp. 65–82). Boston: Boston Research Association for the 21st Century.

Goulah, J., & Ito, T. (2012). Daisaku Ikeda's curriculum of Soka education: Creating value through dialogue, global citizenship, and "human education" in the mentor-disciple relationship. *Curriculum Inquiry, 42*(1), 56–79.

Gundara, J. S., & Sharma, N. (2010). Interculturalism, sustainable development and higher education institutions. *International Journal of Development Education and Global Learning, 2*(2), 23–34.

Henderson, H., & Ikeda, D. (2004). *Planetary citizenship: Your values, beliefs and actions can shape a sustainable world*. Santa Monica, CA: Middleway Press.

Hess, D. E., & McAvoy, P. (2015). *The political classroom: Evidence and ethics in democratic education*. New York: Routledge.

Ikeda, D. (1993). *Mahayana Buddhism and twenty-first century civilization*. Lecture delivered at Harvard University on September 24, 1993. Retrieved from http://www.daisakuikeda.org/sub/resources/works/lect/lect-04.html.

Ikeda, D. (2002).*The challenge of global empowerment: Education for a sustainable future*. Retrieved from http://www.sgi.org/about-us/president-ikedas-proposals/environmental-proposal-2002.html.

Ikeda, D. (2003). *Unlocking the mysteries of birth and death…and everything in between: A Buddhist view of life* (2nd ed.). Santa Monica, CA: Middleway Press.

Ikeda, D. (2008). Thoughts on education for global citizenship. In *My dear friends in America: Collected U.S. addresses 1990–1996* (2nd ed., pp. 441–451). Santa Monica, CA: World Tribune Press.

Ikeda, D. (2014, January 26). 2014 peace proposal. Value creation for global change: Building resilient and sustainable societies. *Soka Gakkai International Newsletter, SGINL 8935*. Retrieved from http://www.sgi.org/content/files/about-us/president-ikedas-proposals/peaceproposal2014.pdf.

Ikeda, D. (2016, May). Selections from SGI President Ikeda's collected works: The wisdom for creating happiness and peace, part 2: Human Revolution, Chapter 17: Message for youth, Part 1 of 4. *Living Buddhism*, 48–55.

Ikegami, K., & Rivalland, C. (2016). Exploring the quality of teacher–child interactions: The Soka discourse in practice. *European Early Childhood Education Research Journal, 24*(4), 1–15. https://doi.org/10.1080/1350293X.2016.1189719.

King, A. (2017, September 18). Neil deGrasse Tyson says it might be "too late" to recover from climate change. *CNN*. Retrieved from http://www.cnn.com/2017/09/17/us/neil-degrasse-tyson-on-climate-change-cnntv/index.html.

Kumar, A. (2008). Development education and dialogic learning in the 21st century. *International Journal of Development Education and Global Learning, 1*(1), 37–48.

Makiguchi, T. (1983). *Jinsei chirigaku* [The geography of human life]. *Makiguchi Tsunesaburo zenshu* [Complete works of Tsunesaburo Makiguchi] (Vols. 1–2). Tokyo: Daisan Bunmeisha.

Morris, L. V. (2008). Higher education and sustainability. *Innovative Higher Education, 32*(179), 180.

Nagashima, J. T. (2016). *The meaning of relationships for student agency in soka education: Exploring the lived experiences and application of Daisaku Ikeda's value-creating philosophy through narrative inquiry*. Unpublished doctoral dissertation, University of Pittsburgh, Pittsburgh, PA.

Oxfam. (2006a). *Education for global citizenship: A guide for schools*. Oxford: Oxfam. Retrieved from http://www.oxfam.org.uk/education/global-citizenship/global-citizenship-guides.

Oxfam. (2006b). *Teaching controversial issues. Global citizenship guides*. Oxford: Oxfam. Retrieved from http://www.oxfam.org.uk/education/global-citizenship/global-citizenship-guides.

Oxfam. (2015). *Education for global citizenship: A guide for schools*. Retrieved from http://www.oxfam.org.uk/education/global-citizenship/global-citizenship-guides.

Reimers, F. M., Chopra, V., Chung, C. K., Higdon, J., & O'Donnell, E. B. (2016). *Empowering global citizens: A world course*. North Charleston, SC: CreateSpace Independent.

Rockefeller, S. C. (2015). *Democratic equality, economic inequality, and the earth charter*. San Jose, Costa Rica: Earth Charter International.

Scheunpflug, A. (2011). Global education and cross-cultural learning: A challenge for a research-based approach to international teacher education. *International Journal of Development Education and Global Learning, 3*(3), 29–44.

Scheunpflug, A. (2012). Identity and ethics in global education: Becoming a global citizen. In L. Jasskelained, T. Kaivola, E. O'Loughlin, & L. Wegimont (Eds.), *Proceedings of the international symposium on competencies of global citizen* (pp. 31–39). Amsterdam: GENE.

Sharma, N. (2008). *Makiguchi and Gandhi: Their educational relevance for the 21st century*. Lanham, MD: University Press of America, Rowman & Littlefield.

Takazawa, M. (2016). *Exploration of soka education principles on global citizenship: A qualitative study of U.S. K-3 soka educators*. Unpublished doctoral dissertation, University of San Francisco, San Francisco. Retrieved from: http://repository.usfca.edu/diss/324.

Takeuchi, K. (2004). The significance of Makiguchi Tsunesaburo's Jinsei Chirigaku (Geography of Human Life) in the intellectual history of geography in Japan: Commemorating the centenary of its publication. *The Journal of Oriental Studies, 14*, 112–132.

Tarozzi, M., & Torres, C. A. (2016). *Global citizenship education and the crises of multiculturalism: Comparative perspectives*. London: Bloomsbury Academic.

UNESCO, International Bureau of Education. (2001, September 5–8). Learning to live together: Have we failed? In *Forty-Sixth Session of UNESCO'S International Conference on Education*. Geneva: UNESCO, International Bureau of Education.

UNESCO, United Nations Educational Scientific and Cultural Organization. (2006). *UNESCO guidelines on intercultural education*. Paris: UNESCO.

UNESCO, United Nations Educational Scientific and Cultural Organization. (2014). *Global citizenship education: Preparing learners for the challenges of the twenty-first century*. Paris: UNESCO.

UNESCO, United Nations Educational Scientific and Cultural Organization. (2015). *Global citizenship education: Topics and learning objectives*. Paris: UNESCO.

UNESCO, United Nations Educational Scientific and Cultural Organization. (2016). *Education 2030: Incheon declaration and framework for action for the implementation of sustainable development goal 4*. Paris: UNESCO.

UNESCO, United Nations Educational, Scientific and Cultural Organization. (2017). *Making textbook content inclusive: A focus on religion, gender, and culture*. Paris: UNESCO.

UNICEF, United Nations Children's Fund. (2013). *Global citizenship: A high school educators guide (grades 9–12)*. Retrieved from www.teachunicef.org.

CHAPTER 7

Culminating Lessons, Moving Forward

Abstract Suggestions are made in this chapter for lessons that engage with Asian thinkers, Mahatma Gandhi, Tsunesaburo Makiguchi, and Daisaku Ikeda's beliefs, modes of thinking, behaviors, and strategies as active protagonists within their respective countries. The proposals made in this chapter are not typical formal lesson plans but include teaching guidelines that can be used to integrate non-Western perspectives to develop a global outlook within teacher education programs; for the professional development of in-service teachers; within undergraduate (bachelor's) and graduate (master's) programs on international and comparative education, development education, and global learning; and within civil society organizations promoting global citizenship education. Core activities are provided that can be used to develop curriculum according to the needs of the cohort.

Keywords Development education and global learning · International and comparative education · Non-Western perspectives · Gandhi Makiguchi · Ikeda

Introduction

The internationalization of higher education and the institutionalization of global citizenship programs within curricula across schools and universities in the world have generated much enthusiasm but have also

N. Sharma, *Value-Creating Global Citizenship Education*,
Palgrave Studies in Global Citizenship Education and Democracy,
https://doi.org/10.1007/978-3-319-78244-7_7

invited criticism from various scholars and groups. For example, within the universities of leading economies that include Australia, the United Kingdom, and the United States, there is a drive to foster globally competent students through study abroad programs, an increased focus on language learning, and other experiences and skills that also aim to enhance the nation's economic competitiveness. Many scholars argue that the current practice of global citizenship further increases the gaps between various people, including the Global North and South, for example, in which cohorts in the South are subjected to various travel restrictions that are not always applicable to the North. This increases the stratification between those who have greater access to mobility compared to those who are confronted by borders and other disparities (see Jooste and Heleta 2017; Rizvi 2007).

In this context, Aktas et al. (2017) recent study examines the different ways of conceptualizing global citizenship in higher education programs while discussing their implications for social justice and equity at both the theoretical and programmatic levels. Taking Shultz's (2007) categorization of the three dominant approaches—neoliberal approach, radical/conflict approach, and critical/transformationalist approach, they analyze a variety of case samples and conclude with recommendations that include, the value of a critical approach as follows,

> In particular, acting critically is an important component of the critical/transformationalist global citizenship approach as it enables cohorts to question global power structures influencing both local and global communities, while opening opportunities for cohorts to reflect on their own place in the world.
>
> (Aktas et al. 2017)

It is also pertinent to add here that for this approach to be used effectively, the knowledge within the curricula should be non-centric and represent diverse perspectives. As argued in Chapter 3, the curricula within schools and university programs should not draw more heavily from one source of knowledge while excluding or marginalizing others. Programs on global citizenship within higher education must also engage with less widely known theories and perspectives.

As in the previous chapter, this chapter as well continues to offer teaching strategies for *learning to live together*. The previous chapter offered themes based on alternative global perspectives as suggestions to reengage with current subjects and courses across schools and higher education. These themes promote the dispositions of criticality and value creation for social-self actualization. In this chapter, the outline for a new course is developed through the study of Makiguchi, Ikeda, and Gandhi. Suggestions are made for lessons that engage with the thinker's beliefs, modes of thinking, behaviors, and strategies for action. The suggested lessons are not formal lesson plans. These are suggestions that can be used to integrate non-Western perspectives to develop a global outlook within teacher education programs; for the professional development of in-service teachers; within undergraduate (bachelors') and graduate (masters') programs on international and comparative education, development education and global learning, future programs on value-creating education for global citizenship; and within civil society organizations promoting global citizenship education. I have provided core activities or teaching strategies that can be used to develop curriculum according to the needs of the cohort.

Lesson Development and Overview

Over the years while studying and working in Higher Education across countries in Asia, Europe, and the United States, I realized that there is a dearth of engagement with non-Western perspectives within learning and teaching. For example, during my schooling experience in Kolkata (Calcutta), India, we read more literary work from Western authors, like William Shakespeare (1564–1616), than the work, for example, of local Bengali poets and playwrights, such as, Rabindranath Tagore (1861–1941) in spite of the extant availability of Tagore's own authored and translated work in English. (The worldwide dominance of the English language as a *lingua franca* might itself be the subject of another discussion.) It was only when I went to Japan and later in UK that I was able to put the emphasis back on Asian thinkers.

It is on the basis of these later personal and professional experiences that the following outline is being offered to develop teaching materials based on the ideas of Makiguchi, Gandhi, and Ikeda. The suggestions below have been written as an outline for a course that can be covered over one semester or extended to a longer length of teaching. The impact will be enhanced when taught within a dialogic and transformative environment where cohorts can interact with the learning materials while bringing their own experiences, values, and aspirations into the classroom.

Overall the course invites cohorts (across programs and academic levels suggested earlier) to explore key debates over the meaning and nature of social justice in global citizenship education, debates that intersect with questions about the person, society, education, and knowledge. Participants are introduced to key concepts, such as citizenship, diversity, equality, globalization, inclusion, power, the state and subjectivity and invited to consider the usefulness of various aspects of these concepts for making sense of education policy and practice.

This study on the Asian thinkers challenges cohorts to read and reflect on their writings (primary sources), to compare texts authored by other scholars on their ideas (secondary sources), and to develop questions related to education for global citizenship. Each unit or module within the proposed course can integrate these successive steps:

1. **watch/read** the assigned material;
2. **reflect** on the materials studied; and
3. work on a culminating **activity/assignment**.

The suggestions in this chapter follow from some of the discussions in Chapters 5 and 6, and include proposals for practice developed through my more recent teaching and curriculum development for global citizenship.

Goals

It is expected that through the successful completion of this course cohorts will:

- be prepared to challenge and question textual material;
- be able to formulate and investigate worthwhile questions related to education for citizenship;
- develop abilities in a broad range of vocational and transferable skills including information gathering, analytical thinking, as well as sustaining and presenting a logical argument in academic writing.

Objectives

By the end of this course, cohorts will have an awareness of:

- the educational ideas of selected Asian thinkers;
- issues that arise in the teaching of values (such as non-violence) and citizenship through a knowledge-based curriculum;
- successful practices of creating change within the untaught curriculum, ethos, and outside curriculum studies; and
- understanding of how the use of value-creating theory can offer benefit in the context of classroom teaching and professional work.

The broader course objectives, based on the conceptual framework of the previous chapters in this book, are to develop:

- knowledge within the course, generated in three main ways: by reflecting on personal experience (for example, through regular entries in a reflective learning journal); through discussion with others (in class or via online forums); and by reading and listening to various educational materials by international scholars (through face-to-face interactions or via the world wide web);
- skills to respond critically to research literature by comparing and evaluating published sources;
- the ability to use libraries and IT resources to search for and acquire relevant information for the purposes of critiquing textual material;
- the ability to work independently to research textual material; and
- the ability to articulate and present an argument in academic writing.

Introduction Lessons

In the icebreaker and introduction week/s it is important to start building a class environment that allows for the teacher and cohorts to bring their interests and aspirations into the classroom. The icebreaker lesson could begin by sharing something that can be related to this course about inspiring people/citizens, for example, generating a discussion about a great person or hero in one's life, and a mentor who made a difference in one's life direction. This can be followed by a short group

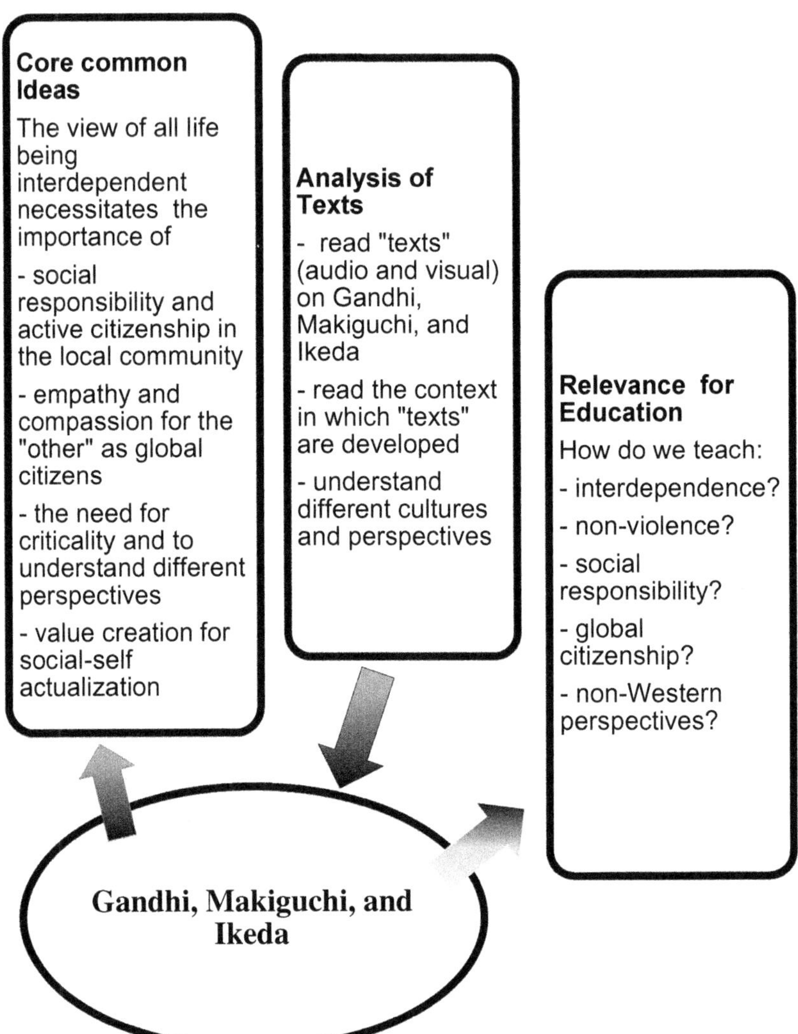

Fig. 7.1 Mind map for a study of Gandhi, Makiguchi, and Ikeda

introduction that includes describing oneself using three or four adjectives, and finally, a discussion centered on two to three learning or course objectives from the course syllabus that might be of particular interest to the students. This activity starts with building engagement between the teachers, cohorts, and learning materials.

Several students who I have taught have never heard the term "global citizen." For an introduction to this course, YouTube videos that students can see before or during class are "Second UNESCO Forum on Global Citizenship Education" and "Global Citizenship is...,"[1] which can be followed by a discussion in class based on the following questions:

- What do you think of the term "global citizen?" Do you agree with this term? Why? Why not?
- Are there any essential elements of a global citizen?
- Can you call yourself a global citizen?

It is important to sensitize students here to the above discussion in this chapter, to the positive and negative images associated with this term, and to critically examine the tendency to associate language study, experience of traveling or study abroad, and the use of technology, as being the determining criteria of a global citizen. Through initial discussions, it is relevant to mention that a close connection to digital technology in itself does not make a person a global citizen. It is, however, useful if social media enhances knowledge, experience, and understanding of other cultures and the wider world (see Bourn 2015).

Figure 7.1 provides an overview of the course that uses textual analysis to examine the key ideas and educational relevance of Gandhi, Makiguchi, and Ikeda.

Lessons on the Thinkers' Life, Work, and Relevance

Lessons on the educational philosophy and practice of the three thinkers can be taught through the use of a historical-comparative study and discussion of non-Western perspectives in education. A three-part historical study can explore (a) their respective historical backgrounds, (b) their personal histories including relevant events and influences on their lives, and (c) their present use and applicability. Overall the method used to study their ideas is based upon a critical, textual, and biographical analysis of their respective lives and values. This involves a study of their writings (primary sources), as well as a comparison of the texts authored by other scholars on their ideas (secondary sources). Primary sources that have been translated need to be read while being mindful of the translator's position and influence on the translated work. Further, the results of the historical-comparative study can shed light on broader issues that are relevant to educating citizens in the twenty-first century. For example, students can examine the use of their ideas in selected schools through both the taught and untaught curriculum. In the case of Makiguchi and Ikeda, it can be a sample from the Soka Schools (where Ikeda is the founder) and non-Soka Schools (established by others who are inspired by the *soka* or value-creating pedagogy and philosophy). As a culminating activity, students can analyze the relevance of the core ideas and themes that emerge for a study and application of global citizenship education within their own particularities, schools, and communities.

The following questions can be used to guide a more detailed engagement with these thinkers, their ideas, movements, and relevance for global citizenship education (developed from Sharma 2008):

1. **What are the key contradictions and paradoxes which can be identified in a contextual and historical analysis of their value systems?** This question guides an investigation of the context in which these thinkers were placed. It also draws us to engage with their writings/texts, and to understand the time and context in which these were written.[2]
2. **How have the "values" systems or values and beliefs of the thinkers impacted upon education today?** This question guides an investigation into the use and influence of their ideas in education and examines the applicability of their proposals.
3. **Is there any way in which the findings of this analysis may have generalizable use for future studies?** This question engages with the outcomes from a study on these thinkers that need further investigation, for example, identification of their strategies, behaviors, and beliefs as citizens.

To summarize, as the sessions progress students should be able to critically engage with various issues within global citizenship education across the international community as well as to understand that education needs to be sensitive to the culture of the students, school, and community.

Lessons on the Thinkers' Life and Work in the Twentieth Century

Gandhi's Life and Work in the Twentieth Century

A study of Gandhi's life and work in twentieth century India can include an introduction to Gandhi, his core ideas, and identification with some of his successes and challenges as a national leader. As part of the learning outcomes students can

- understand the meaning of key words and phrases used within Gandhi's movement for Indian independence (including *satya*, *ahimsa*, and *satyagraha*—see the glossary);
- analyze and explain Gandhi's ideas within the context in which these were developed;
- compare ideas in primary and secondary texts to understand different perspectives;
- develop knowledge of Gandhi's philosophy and movement for Indian independence.

The introduction to Gandhi can be through a short film on Gandhi's biography[3] followed by a more multilayered analysis of the influences on Gandhi that includes a study of his choice of influence, for example, his intentional use of the Indian attire, language, and culture within his political movement (as discussed in Chapters 2 and 5). The introduction to Gandhi should also take a critical and analytical approach to secondary source writings that comment on his personal history.

A core activity should engage students in readings on Gandhi's concept of *ahimsa* or non-violence and its use (through primary and secondary sources—as examples see Gandhi 1939; Hardiman 2003: 59; Sharma 2008: 69). Questions can include,

- how is Gandhi's view, that even Hitler could be won over by non-violence, interpreted differently in each text?
- how did you respond to the argument made in each text?

Guiding points should help students to organize their own thoughts about the extent to which each of these texts about *ahimsa* deal with the issue differently, and how it gives them a different perspective on the use of non-violence in politics and daily life.

A follow up reflective question for the journal entry can be "why are contradictions and paradoxes likely to emerge when 'values' are confronted with the reality of politics?" Students should respond to this critical question in the journal based on their study of Gandhi. It is important here that students develop an understanding of the various aspects of Gandhi, the moral, radical, and creative leader, and of the scale of non-violent mass movement as exemplary in human history that galvanized a disparate community.

Makiguchi's Life and Work in the Twentieth Century

Similar to the study on Gandhi, a critical analysis of Makiguchi's historical background, personal history, and educational ideas can be developed to get clarity on Makiguchi as the humanistic educator but also to shed light on his creativity within education, and as a champion of human rights who staked his life on his beliefs.

An important aspect to bring into the classroom discussion is the aim of happiness as the goal of education. For Makiguchi, the aim of education should be derived from the aim of life, which as he found, was that everyone ultimately desires to lead a happy life. Several scholars have distinguished this from the concept of pleasure (Norton in Bethel 1989: 207–208; Kumagai 1994: 69–74). According to Makiguchi, a life of happiness is one in which value can be created that is useful for life, for social-self actualization.[4]

As examined earlier in Chapters 2 and 6, Makiguchi's educational proposals centered on the idea that through leading a contributive life an individual can create value that can benefit both self (through creating the value of the benefit or personal gain) and others (through social good). A focus on Makiguchi's life and work should include the following aspects,

- for students to be able to recognize and articulate keywords and phrases in research on Makiguchi's educational theory (including *soka*, Soka, and *ningen kyoiku* as elaborated upon in Chapters 1 and 2);
- the concept of value creation as relationship building within education (see Chapter 6); and
- the home-school-community continuum for the development of the learner.

Ikeda's Life and Work in the Twentieth Century
Similar to the study on Gandhi and Makiguchi, a critical analysis of Ikeda's historical background, personal history, and educational ideas should be developed. The two key aspects to engage within a study on Ikeda's ideas for global citizenship are (as discussed in Chapters 2 and 4),

- his proposals on education for global citizenship and sustainability;
- the contribution of a study on his life and work to revisiting the role of dialogue and dialogic processes of learning in global citizenship education.

Resource materials include,

- Ikeda's 1996 lecture presented at Teachers College, Columbia University, New York on the topic of education for global citizenship (Ikeda 2008);
- proposals to the United Nations[5] (including, Ikeda 2014);
- the discourse on Ikeda's dialogue, and scholarly work on the use of the term "dialogue" within *soka*/Ikeda studies (Goulah 2012).

A culminating activity for assessment can be a response paper that analyzes the film, *Another way of seeing things*,[6] based on an essay by Ikeda. In this essay, Ikeda challenges media stereotyping and how this can give rise to prejudice and barriers between people of different nationalities and religions. Students can be asked to see the film at least two times. The following questions can be circulated after they have seen the film once, and before they view it again.

- What is the main topic or problem being addressed? In your own words state what the film is about.
- What is the argument being made in this film?
- What evidence is provided in support of the argument?
- Is there an alternative argument to be made?
- How did you find yourself responding to the text on first reading? How did you find yourself responding after considering these questions?

Lessons Focused on Their Relevance for the Twenty-First Century

One of the aims of this study is to seek the present day relevance of Gandhi, Makiguchi, and Ikeda through a historical study. We can learn from all three thinkers' creativity and active participation in their respective local communities and societies. This study has implications for education for citizenship.

The Relevance of Gandhi and Ahimsa to Global Citizenship Education
Through lessons developed on this topic students will be able to:

- analyze the use and relevance of Gandhi's *ahimsa* in our present time;
- reflect on how intercultural understanding or knowledge of other cultures is a key attribute for citizens across diverse communities;
- recognize the benefits of a historical, contextual study for classroom teaching;
- identify and explain how Gandhi's ideas have been used and misused since his death.

Three main aspects that need to be considered in Gandhi's presence and absence within India today (as discussed in Chapter 2; also see Sharma 2008: 95–104) are,

1. some of the challenges in adopting his ideas;
2. the limitations of the present state education systems;
3. dissension among his successors.

As a group, students should discuss and shed light on various aspects that need consideration in teaching and practicing Gandhi's ideas, such as, his understanding of *ahimsa* or non-violence, within the school curriculum. For example, the subject matter or lesson content should include the context in which Gandhi developed his views on non-violence, the aims of the lesson, the methods that can be used to teach non-violence, the philosophy of the school in which this is taught, the culture and politics of the country in which the school exists, and the teacher's own experiences and views on this subject. In addition to teaching about Gandhi and non-violence, there is also the opportunity to think of broader issues that concern the students and institutions in which the learning takes place. For example, think of the culture of violence within societies, and how Gandhi's ideas end up being negotiated (for example, with reference to different ways in which his ideas have sometimes been used as discussed in Chapter 2).

It is important to be mindful as mentioned earlier that while engaging with the moral aspects of Gandhi as the *Mahatma* (or great soul), students also need to engage with Gandhi's strategies, behaviors, and beliefs as an active protagonist within his nation's history.

The Relevance of Soka Praxis to Global Citizenship Education

As for Gandhi, three main aspects should be considered to study the absence and presence of Makiguchi in Japan (see Sharma 2008: Chapter 6; also key issues discussed in Chapter 2). These are:

1. the challenges in adopting some of his ideas which were developed for the context in which he taught;
2. the limitations of the present education system;
3. the establishment of Soka institutions by Ikeda.

This includes an engagement with the practical application of value-creating education across examples from the Soka and non-Soka institutions located across the world that is each impacted by local and global factors. The broader goals should be to form reflective questions in relation to the taught and untaught aspects of the curriculum, and to recognize various influences that impact education in schools.

A core activity should be to engage with the negative and positive impacts of the hidden curriculum and untaught curriculum within schools. This includes, an examination of the Soka Schools in Japan as a positive example of educating students as "global citizens" through the untaught curriculum, ethos, and outside curriculum studies (see Chapter 6 in Sharma 2008; Gerbert and Joffee 2007 for a succinct reading of key issues), and other materials that discuss negative examples of hidden curriculum.[7]

Contribution of Non-Western Perspectives To Reimagining Education for Citizenship

The concluding lesson/s captures key learning from this study. The examination of Gandhi, Makiguchi, and Ikeda's lives and ideas draws our attention to Asian perspectives in education. Further, materials can be used to engage with diverse perspectives and to develop an understanding of our interdependence as humanity, for example, through videos that engage with the impact of events such as 9/11 on school curricula.[8] In using this or similar materials, guiding questions as concluding discussions can include:

- "Your thoughts from the video and other resources studied in class on why learning about an interdependent world is considered as being relevant in education today?"
- "How can theories of interdependence, Western and non-Western, enhance learning within the curriculum content as well as the untaught curriculum?"
- "How, if so, can we measure the impact of the untaught curriculum on a student's academic achievement and overall well being?"

The three guiding key questions stated earlier in this chapter can be used to re-engage with essential points covered in this study. To reiterate,

1. What are the key contradictions and paradoxes which can be identified in a contextual and historical analysis of Gandhi, Makiguchi, and Ikeda's value systems?
2. How have the "values" systems or values and beliefs of the thinkers impacted upon education today?
3. Is there any way in which the findings of this analysis may have generalizable use for future studies?

Questions discussed in Chapter 5 can be used to wrap up the course. Final assessments could include participation in a group project and an individual response paper to an assigned journal article. These culminating activities can be used to argue the relevance of studying non-Western perspectives within global citizenship education.

Notes

1. https://www.youtube.com/watch?v=GtRrV1H_4yY and https://www.youtube.com/watch?v=XVSgbU6WVSk.
2. See this video that takes Gandhi as an example to show why contextualization is an essential skill: https://www.teachingchannel.org/videos/reading-like-a-historian-contextualization.
3. https://www.biography.com/people/mahatma-gandhi-9305898.

4. For key lines of thought within Makiguchi's work see Sharma (2008: 53–61).
5. http://www.daisakuikeda.org/main/peacebuild/peace-proposals/pp2017.html.
6. It is the winner of the 2004 Chris Award, Columbus International Film Festival and is included in the book (Ikeda 2005).
7. https://www.theguardian.com/society/2004/apr/30/publichealth.comment.
8. https://www.youtube.com/watch?v=GCYCNn3qOyk.

References

Aktas, F., Pitts, K., Richards, J. C., & Iveta, S. (2017). Institutionalizing global citizenship: A critical analysis of higher education programs and curricula. *Journal of Studies in International Education, 21*(1), 65–80.

Bethel, D. M. (Ed.). (1989). *Education for creative living: Ideas and proposals of Tsunesaburo Makiguchi*. Ames: Iowa State University Press.

Bourn, D. (2015). *Global citizenship and youth participation in Europe- report*. Schools for Future Use and Erasmus. Retrieved from http://sfyouth.eu/index.php/en/mm-about-en/reports/needanalysis.

Gandhi, M. K. (1939, October 25). Discussion with executive members of Gandhi Seva Sangh Wardha. In *The collected works of Mahatma Gandhi*. Retrieved from http://www.gandhiserve.org/cwmg/VOL077.PDF.

Gebert, A., & Joffee, M. (2007). Value creation as the aim of education: Tsunesaburo Makiguchi and Soka education. In D. T. Hansen (Ed.), *Ethical visions of education: Philosophies in practice* (pp. 65–82). New York: Teachers College Press. Retrieved from http://www.tmakiguchi.org/assets/images/Gebert_Joffee_rw_090120.pdf.

Goulah, J. (2012). Daisaku Ikeda and value-creative dialogue: A new current in interculturalism and educational philosophy. *Educational Philosophy and Theory, 44*(9), 997–1009. https://doi.org/10.1111/j.1469-5812.2011.00827.x.

Hardiman, D. (2003). *Gandhi: In his time and ours*. New Delhi: Permanent Black.

Ikeda, D. (2005). *One by one: The world is yours to change*. Sonoma, CA: Dunhill Publishing.

Ikeda, D. (2008). Thoughts on education for global citizenship. In *My dear friends in America: Collected U.S. addresses 1990–1996* (2nd ed., pp. 441–451). Santa Monica, CA: World Tribune Press.

Ikeda, D. (2014, January 26). 2014 peace proposal. Value creation for global change: Building resilient and sustainable societies. *Soka Gakkai International Newsletter, SGINL 8935*. Retrieved from http://www.sgi.org/content/files/about-us/president-ikedas-proposals/peaceproposal2014.pdf.

Jooste, N., & Heleta, S. (2017). Global citizenship versus globally competent graduates: A critical view from the South. *Journal of Studies in International Education, 21*(1), 39–51.

Kumagai, K. (1994). *Soka kyoikugaku nyumon* [An introduction to Soka/value-creating education pedagogy]. Tokyo: Daisanbunmeisha.

Rizvi, F. (2007). Internationalization of curriculum: A critical perspective. In M. Hayden, J. Levy, & J. Thompson (Eds.), *Research in international education* (pp. 391–403). London: Sage.

Sharma, N. (2008). *Makiguchi and Gandhi: Their educational relevance for the 21st century.* Lanham, MD: University Press of America, Rowman & Littlefield.

Shultz, L. (2007). Educating for global citizenship: Conflicting agendas and understandings. *Alberta Journal of Educational Research, 53,* 248–258.

CHAPTER 8

Conclusions—Recommendations for Policy and Practice

Abstract In this concluding chapter, Sharma brings together the core learning within this book on Asian perspectives for a value-creating global citizenship education that can expand the current emphasis on individual empowerment to a more collective focus on creating value for social-self actualization. This chapter offers suggestions for researchers and practitioners who are interested in pursuing Gandhi studies, Makiguchi/Ikeda/*soka* studies, and the integration of less widely known perspectives into the discourse and praxis within global citizenship education. Recommendations are made for policy and practice based on the various strands and elements discussed in this work.

Keywords Global citizenship education · Learning to live together Soka education · Makiguchi · Ikeda · Gandhi

It is hoped that readers will continue the conversations through the blog available via this link: https://vcgce.wordpress.com which also offers suggestions for further readings on *Gandhi's education and practice of non-violence*; *Makiguchi's value-creating pedagogy*; and *Ikeda's essays and lectures on humanistic education.*

N. Sharma, *Value-Creating Global Citizenship Education*,
Palgrave Studies in Global Citizenship Education and Democracy,
https://doi.org/10.1007/978-3-319-78244-7_8

A Shift in Emphasis

Value-creating global citizenship education expands the current focus on individual empowerment and collaboration, to enhance the possibilities for a creative coexistence. For instance, it proposes a shift in emphasis within the three domains of learning as currently described for the practice of global citizenship education by UNESCO (2015), from critical thinking within the cognitive domain to dialogue and dialogic modes of learning, from empathy and consideration of others within the socio-emotional domain to friendship and compassion, and from charity and advocacy within the behavioral dimension to enhancing value creation for self and others (see Chapters 4–6).

There are three important aspects for policy and practice to consider. The first is the importance of developing an intercultural lens that accommodates the multiple layers of identities of citizens within national and global communities. This is particularly crucial so that education for global citizenship can develop inclusive citizens, whose faith, cultural dispositions, and other values are seen as being integral to effectively fulfilling their role as citizens. Learning in the classroom should therefore engage with the values of the learner as emphasized in previous chapters of this book. Second, is to adopt a value-creating approach that is based on the understanding that acquiring subject knowledge does not mean that a student would also develop the ability to live contributively. This book has started to engage with some important discussions on philosophy, pedagogy, teaching methods, and tools that place an emphasis on developing relationships within education. The third key aspect is to consider the contributions that Asian and less widely known ideas and approaches can make to this field. For instance, Gandhi's vision for independent India was based on a decentralized framework of governance which was disregarded and instead modern India adopted a centralized socio-political structure with a constitution that was framed largely on the basis of Anglo-Saxon principles. As briefly discussed earlier in this book, the notion of duties and rights that emerge from both frameworks are vastly different. Policy makers and practitioners should particularize global citizenship education to their respective local and national contexts.

The chosen thinkers proposed alternative ways of thinking, being, and acting based on which this book promotes the notions of a creative citizen, an inclusive citizen, and an active citizen. It contributes to the discourse on global citizenship with the aim to foster planetary citizens who are equipped with the value-creating capacity for social-self actualization, who possess wisdom derived from knowledge, and have the courage and compassion to perceive the world as a cosmic living entity, while also being able to critically challenge power and structural inequities at various levels.

For future work in the field of Gandhi studies for global citizenship, a more detailed examination of movements in which Gandhi's influence can be delineated can contribute to the goals of education for non-violence, sustainable development, and intercultural education within global citizenship. It is also imperative to engage with all facets of Gandhi and his work as outlined in previous discussions, the moral Gandhi, the radical Gandhi, and the creative Gandhi that would allow (particularly older) students to engage in challenging conversations about issues such as gun laws in countries like the United States and the "good guy with a gun" theory that the National Rifle Association (NRA) and others use to justify their position. The time to talk about the systems and culture that perpetuate violence is now, and while UNESCO has a specific theme to prevent violent extremism, it also needs to engage with violence within societies, for example, as a well developed theme that is accompanied with a teacher's guide and resources for the classroom. This is the kind of task that can be done under the auspices of UNESCO MGIEP (Mahatma Gandhi Institute of Education for Peace and Sustainable Development) in India through a robust engagement with Gandhi, whose reference currently has been reduced by the Institute to the abstract notion of "Gandhi neurons."[1]

For *soka*/Ikeda studies a comprehensive analysis is needed of the conceptual foundations of Ikeda's ideas that have motivated citizens, especially the youth across diverse nation states. As an example, as stated earlier (in Chapters 2 and 7), the framework used for my study on Makiguchi and Gandhi is offered toward such a project. To reiterate, an interdisciplinary methodology should be developed to locate his ideas (examining sociological, pedagogical, and political issues), his effectiveness as a citizen within his own historical context, and the impact on education and civic movements. Three historical readings can be used to interpret his relevance. First, a history of the era and time that provides a contextual setting for studying his life; second, the specific events and influences that shaped his personal history and led to the formation of his value systems; and the third should be concerned with a re-reading of the use of his ideas and values within the twenty-first century context.

One of the outcomes of such a detailed study would lead to a comprehensive analysis of the conceptual foundations of Ikeda's ideas, values, and modes of thinking. To summarize, this study would lead to an examination of Ikeda as a historical actor, his creativity as analyzed by contextualizing his contributions from within his historical locale, as well as his influence within different communities and countries, within the particularities of selected schools and on youth and education.

Comparative research in *soka* studies should not be seen as a compromise of the original intent of the progenitors of *soka* as such studies can further develop the relevance of universal ideals within particularities. For instance, future research can examine the origins of public education in Europe during the Age of Enlightenment in comparison to the Buddhist concept of enlightenment. For example, its influence on the ancient Buddhist sites of learning that was catered for the wider Indian polity, as well as the more recent examples of the Soka educational institutions worldwide that focus on student's happiness and developing their abilities to live contributively.

Similarly, within the field of *soka* studies a thorough engagement with existing and emerging scholarly work can generate a more substantial discourse. This would also help to elucidate the field, for example, developing a clearer examination of the present loosely used term "Soka education," an understanding of *ningen kyoiku* and Ikeda's vision for humanistic education. For *soka*/Makiguchi/Ikeda studies, as mentioned in Chapters 1 and 2, the use of key terms and concepts within emerging studies can strengthen the discourse in this field. Also, there needs to be some circumspection in using words, such as, "Ikedian," in light of the negative and contextual use of thinkers, such as Gandhi, as exemplified through the terms "Gandhian" and "Gandhism." As mentioned earlier (in Chapter 2), in India such terms have often been invoked, used or disregarded suited to the context of those who speak of Gandhi. On the subject of Gandhian and Gandhism, Gandhi himself is known to remark,

> I do not know myself who is a Gandhian. Gandhism is a meaningless word for me. As ism follows the propounder of a system. I am not one, hence I cannot be the cause of an ism. If an ism is built up it will not endure and if it does it will not be Gandhism.
>
> (Iyer 1991: 62)

Similarly, "Ikedian-ism" or an "Ikedian-system" would do disservice to the creative modes of thinking of Ikeda himself as well as the creativity that he has sought to foster within the particularities, specificities, and needs of people, education, and communities.

Further, many scholars and Soka Gakkai International members recognize the influence of *soka* ethos within the Soka schools, university, and the Buddhist organization. As an example, through their own experiences of being inspired by reading Ikeda's writings many teacher practitioners have positively enhanced their teaching styles and attitudes. The significance of the transformation or "human revolution" of the teacher is admirable and indispensable to creating a meaningful change within education and society (see Chapters 4 and 6). At the same time, there is substantive academic research work being carried out on the educational ideas of the progenitors of *soka* (for example through translation and comparative studies) that needs to be disseminated for a wider readership, making publications and literature more accessible in order to engage with and enhance the teacher's practice of *soka* principles within the classroom.

A much broader applicability of value-creating global citizenship education needs to examine how the creation of value can take place not only within teaching and education but also in other areas within the lived experiences of people's daily lives.

The following recommendations are made for national, local, and institutional policy makers, especially given the perpetuation of inequities and inequalities that continue through economic policies that support the "neoliberal ideology" (Hamdon and Jorgenson 2011: 264). In education these neoliberal principles based policies advocate for the privatization of public institutions, promote individualism, and benefit privileged minorities at national and global levels (Hamdon and Jorgenson 2011). Here, supplementary perspectives can offer innovative ways to re-think policy and practice for global citizenship. As a start, the goal of *learning to live together* would necessitate having difficult conversations about race and identity starting from the policy level (as discussed in Chapter 4 taking examples from citizenship education in UK). The changing representation of Gandhi and non-violence within the history textbooks in India is also an example of how the curriculum has been framed by political intent.

The dominance of English as the *lingua franca* in developing and promoting global citizenship education worldwide makes it particularly important that curricular themes and practices can allow learning from other views that are developed within non-English and/or non-Western contexts. At a basic level, three rights that need to be guaranteed for all children that emerge from the study in this book are, first, the right to a non-centric curriculum—that allows learning from diverse knowledge and wisdom, second, the right to fulfill one's unique potential—an inside-out and bottom-up approach to education for global citizenship that is transformative and adapts to particularities, and third, the right to a safe learning environment—that fosters the courage to conquer prejudice and violence.

Finally, as discussed in Chapter 5, scholars like Rorty (1998) suggest small campaigns over movements since the latter is described as often being ineffective and self-contradictory in the long term. However, this book elucidates the importance of the role of Soka as a movement similar to *satyagraha* in terms of enthusing a diverse group of people to take positive action within their local communities. As mentioned, personal values can be of benefit not only to the individual but also to the society at large, as long as the use of values is educationally oriented with a focus on the political education of the members who in turn hold the political powers accountable.

In global citizenship education whereas the emphasis has been on charity, youth and advocacy, there also needs to be an understanding of ways in which people and youth are connecting on key concerns within the twenty-first century. The engagement of citizens across nation states on issues, such as, women and sexual abuse, human rights and democracy, transgender issues, and the different ways in which cultures and identities are being shaped through social media are among examples of how people and youth are inspired to create positive global change. Policy makers across nation states can help to promote such aspirations as well as initiatives, such as by civil society organizations like the Soka Gakkai and its youth-led campaigns for the abolition of nuclear weapons (see Chapter 5).

Learning: The Treasure Within

In my own concluding thoughts when teaching I often end with this Buddhist parable. One of the important lessons from the non-Western perspectives studied in this book can be explained by the example of this parable of "The jewel hidden in the robe."[2]

Once upon a time there lived a man who had, as a friend, a rich public servant. One day the man called on his rich friend, who entertained him with food and wine. He became completely inebriated and fell asleep. The rich friend, however, suddenly had to set out on a journey involving urgent public business. He wanted to give his friend a priceless jewel which had the mystic power to fulfill any desire. But his friend was fast asleep. Finding no other alternative, he sewed the gem into the hem of his sleeping friend's robe. The man awoke to find his friend gone, totally unaware of the jewel his friend had given him. Before long, he allowed himself to sink into poverty, wandering through many countries and experiencing many hardships. After a long time, now reduced to a state of sheer want, he met his old friend. The rich man, surprised at his condition, told him about the gift he had given him, and the man learned for the first time that he had possessed the priceless jewel all along.

This is an allegory that reminds us of the vast inner potential that exists within ourselves and others. For education it means paying attention to not just the knowledge content in classroom teaching, but also giving adequate attention to the institution's untaught curriculum. Such a qualitative approach to knowledge and values places importance on developing trust and a sense of purpose in the youth.

In conclusion to this book I would like to raise the two aspects of the "the treasure within" as represented in the Delors Report (1996). The first is the treasure that lies within human beings, the abilities and aptitudes that can enhance social-self actualization. The second is the value of learning itself as the treasure, which been championed as the right of each child by activists such as the Nobel Prize laureate Malala Yousafzai (b. 1997). In responding to the second aspect of perceiving education as a "treasure," the broader emphasis is on developing societies that values and supports the *needs of education*.

The first aspect has led to much emphasis being placed on Project-based Learning (PBL), theatre and arts based approach, and the development of video games within the recent practice of global citizenship education. While such experiential learning methods are important, it is also equally crucial to engage with the existing experiences, values, needs, and interests that the learners bring into the classroom from their home and community. In my personal experience I can say that although I have learned much through the education I received at various schools and universities, it was largely my daily subjective experiences in my family and community that have propelled the development of my work and the endeavor for a meaningful life. These include my interactions with Ikeda and study at Soka University, as well as the indirect experience of Gandhi and the Indian independence movement as the daughter of a once refugee who experienced the partition of undivided India (on August 15, 1947), and as a great granddaughter of a victim of the Jallianwala Bagh massacre (on April 13, 1919), an incident that killed innocent non-violent protestors who were rallying for Indian independence.

In engaging with youth through teaching, within families and communities, the meaningful questions that become pertinent are: what motivates this youth, enthuses her, interests him, and captivates their imagination? I believe that in engaging with these questions education for global citizenship can continue to place the focus on the happiness of learners, the citizens of this world.

Notes

1. As in the video link made available via http://mgiep.unesco.org.
2. http://www.sgi.org/about-us/president-ikedas-writings/the-jewel-hidden-in-the-robe.html.

References

Delors, J., et al. (1996). *Learning: The treasure within*. Paris: UNESCO.

Hamdon, E., & Jorgenson, S. (2011). Policy implications for global citizenship education in higher education in an age of neo-liberalism. In L. Shultz, A. A. Abdi, & G. H. Richardson (Eds.), *Global citizenship education in post-secondary institutions: Theories, practices, and policies* (pp. 260–272). New York: Peter Lang.

Iyer, R. (Ed.). (1991). *The essential writings of Mahatma Gandhi*. Oxford: Oxford University Press.

Rorty, R. (1998). *Achieving our country: Leftist thought in twentieth-century America*. Cambridge, MA: Harvard University Press.

UNESCO, United Nations Educational Scientific and Cultural Organization. (2015). *Global citizenship education: Topics and learning objectives*. Paris: UNESCO.

Glossary

Glossary of Indian (Mostly Hindi and Sanskrit) Terms

Ahimsa Non-injury, non-violence, harmlessness; renunciation of the will to kill and the intention to hurt; abstention from any hostile thought, word, or act; non-coercion

Ashram A spiritual fellowship or community

Bapu Father (often as a form of address)

Charkha Spinning wheel (used by Gandhi to make the *khadi* cloth)

***Chipko* movement** A forest conservation movement that started in 1970s India by a follower of Gandhi, in which non-violent protestors clung to the trees to prevent them from being destroyed

Dharma Duty, righteousness, moral law; social and personal morality; natural law, natural obligation

Jati Indicates grouping among Hindus that are exclusive and endogamous; associated with job function, religious beliefs, or language; a form of existence determined by birth

Kala pani lit. black waters; a taboo on Indian expatriates from seventeenth to nineteenth centuries, causing a loss of one's social class according to some Hindu texts

N. Sharma, *Value-Creating Global Citizenship Education*,
Palgrave Studies in Global Citizenship Education and Democracy,
https://doi.org/10.1007/978-3-319-78244-7

Karuna karuṇā (in both Sanskrit and Pali) is generally translated as compassion; a fundamental quality in Jainism, Hinduism, and the bodhisattva ideal of Mahayana Buddhism; the word comes from the Sanskrit *kara* (Hindi *karna*) meaning "to do" or "to make," indicating an action-based form of compassion, rather than the pity or sadness associated with the English word

Khadi Hand-spun and hand-woven cloth

Kurta (***kurti*** for women), a traditional piece of clothing, a loose shirt falling either just above or somewhere below the knees of the wearer, worn in northern India, Pakistan, and Afghanistan

Lungi A two meter length of cloth worn by men on the lower half of the body and looks like a sarong, found in parts of India, Bangladesh and Myanmar

Mahatma Great soul; name given to Gandhi by the Indian poet Rabindranath Tagore (1861–1941)

Metta The Buddhist virtue of kindness, meditation focused on the development of unconditional love for all beings, from Pali mētta "loving-kindness"; includes the element of unconditional love

Raj Kingdom, rule, regime

Sangha (Sanskrit "Samgha") Community, association, assembly, or company; in Buddhism it refers to the monastic community; also described as a community of friends practicing the *dharma* together

Satya Truth; real, existent; valid; sincere, pure; effectual

Satyagraha Non-violent resistance; a relentless search for truth; truth-force; holding on to truth; the name of Gandhi's political movement

Satyagrahi One who offers *satyagraha*

Swaraj Freedom; self-rule; political independence

Vasudhaiva Kutumbakam A Sanskrit phrase meaning "the whole world is one family"

Glossary of Japanese Terms

Gakkai Society; can be used for academic societies; short form of Soka Gakkai

Jihi Compassion, in Buddhism *ji* means giving happiness and *hi* means saving sentient beings from suffering; includes the element of unconditional love

Komeito A political party in Japan organized in 1964, part of the ruling coalition, political endorsement is provided by the Soka Gakkai

Meiji era The time period from 1868 until 1912 (named after Emperor Meiji)

Mombusho Ministry of Education (now MEXT: Ministry of Education, Culture, Sports, Science and Technology)

Soka Or "value creation" is a neology formed by Josei Toda (1900–1958) to describe Makiguchi's educational pedagogy

Soka Gakkai "Value-Creating Society' is a lay people organization of the Nichiren Shoshu sect of Mahayana Buddhism. It is successor to the organization established by Tsunesaburo Makiguchi in 1930 known as the "Soka Kyoiku Gakkai" or Value-Creating Education Society. Josei Toda reconstructed the organization after the Second World War. Makiguchi is considered as the first president of the Soka Gakkai, Josei Toda was the second president, and Daisaku Ikeda is the third and current president of the Soka Gakkai and the founding president of the Soka Gakkai International (SGI)

Taisho The time period from 1912 to 1926 (coinciding with the reign of the emperor Taisho)

Index

N. Sharma, *Value-Creating Global Citizenship Education*, Palgrave Studies in Global Citizenship Education and Democracy, https://doi.org/10.1007/978-3-319-78244-7

Printed by Printforce, the Netherlands